ProjectThink

ProjectThink

Why Good Managers Make Poor Project Choices

LEV VIRINE AND MICHAEL TRUMPER

GOWER

Published by
Gower Publishing Limited
Wey Court East
Union Road
Farnham
Surrey, GU9 7PT
England

Ashgate Publishing Company
110 Cherry Street
Suite 3-1
Burlington, VT 05401-3818
USA

www.gowerpublishing.com

British Library Cataloguing in Publication Data
Virine, Lev, 1964-
 ProjectThink : why good managers make poor project choices.
 1. Project management--Decision making.
 I. Title II. Trumper, Michael, 1963-
 658.4'04-dc23

Library of Congress Cataloging-in-Publication Data
Virine, Lev, 1964-
 ProjectThink : why good managers make poor project choices / by Lev Virine and Michael Trumper.
    pages cm
 Includes bibliographical references and index.
  ISBN 978-1-4094-5498-4 (hardback) -- ISBN 978-1-4094-5499-1 (ebook) -- ISBN 978-1-4724-0403-9 (epub) 1. Project management--Decision making. 2. Project management. 3. Decision making. I. Trumper, Michael, 1963- II. Title.
  HD69.P75V5683 2013
  658.4'03--dc23

2012049716

ISBN 9781409454984 (hbk)
ISBN 9781409454991 (ebk – PDF)
ISBN 9781472404039 (ebk – ePUB)

FSC
www.fsc.org
MIX
Paper from
responsible sources
FSC® C013985

Printed in the United Kingdom by Henry Ling Limited, at the Dorset Press, Dorchester, DT1 1HD

Contents

PART III: PROJECT ANALYSIS VS. MENTAL ERRORS

PART IV: CHOICE ENGINEERING

List of Figures

List of Tables

Preface

Project management is the art and science of human interactions performed by one group of people to meet other people's needs. The overwhelming majority of problems in projects are due to the unforeseen consequences of intentional or unintentional human actions. People make poor estimates, forget something, communicate poorly, or make other seemingly small mistakes that conspire together and lead to larger issues. This book is about how good and experienced project managers make bad choices and what should they do to avoid it.

Why do individuals and groups consistently repeat the same mistakes? Take a moment to look at the pyramid on the cover of this book. Which square is darker: A or B? Most people believe that B is darker, although both colors are identical. People consistently make mistakes because of differences in the way each of us perceives things – difference which lead to faulty judgment and poor decisions.

Project management processes are established to smooth out differences in both processes and perception with the aim to reducing mistakes and avoiding nasty surprises. A few years ago, we wrote a book on project decision-making, *Project Decisions: The Art and Science* (Virine and Trumper 2007). We described a formal project decision-making process intended to improve the quality of project managers' decisions. The problem is processes are hard to establish and follow, and are rarely followed consistently unless great effort is taken to maintain them. The experience shows that these processes do need to be flexible.

And processes, while they encourage consistency, are a fundamentally inefficient way of trying to align how people think and behave. There is a less expensive and a more flexible way to avoid the negative impact of differences in perception and misplaced decisions. It is possible to create *an environment in which people make better choices without mandating these choices.* Think about the common speed bump. Instead of having to waste the police's time monitoring speed, speed bumps encourage people to make a good choice, in this case, limiting their speed. People choose to slow down not because somebody might give them a ticket, but because it is more comfortable and easier on their vehicles. Project management processes need to be *policed*, but an environment for making better choices can be *engineered*. Speed bumps are engineered to continually steer people towards better choices. Project managers frequently use techniques that collectively are called choice engineering in many industries – sometimes without even knowing it. In most projects, process policing and choice engineering make for very effective partners.

A major component of choice engineering is education – learning how cognitive differences affect human decision-making. In Part I of the book you will learn fundamental concepts about choice engineering. In Part II of this book you will learn about memory, emotions, biases, happiness, and how they can create mental errors and traps. Understanding how these affect your judgment will help you to make better choices. Part III of the book focuses on analysis: you will learn how to analyze information and risks in such a manner to minimize the effect of these mental errors. In Part IV we will provide some advice and techniques to enable you to set up choice engineering as part of your project management environment.

This book is for anybody who is involved in projects. The book doesn't involve learning formulas or understanding complex analyses. What we hope it does is help you discover some key things about yourself and people around you.

Lev Virine and Michael Trumper
Calgary, Alberta, Canada

Test Your Judgment

Here is a quiz to test your judgment as a project manager. This is not an IQ test so don't feel embarrassed if you don't answer some of the questions. As you will learn from this book, judgment of all people is affected by various illusions. However, if you know how to mitigate the negative impact of these illusions, you would make better choices. Consider this exercise an introduction to the book. We will discuss the problems from the test along with other issues throughout the book.

1. Conrad White, the former CFO of Efron Inc., having served time for fraud and embezzlement, now needs to decide on a career. Which project should bring him more value?

    a) Accept the invitation of his prison buddy Robin Hoode and rob the bank at Parkland Blvd. and 10th St. The chance of being caught is 80%. Potential payout is $200,000.

    b) Become an Autumnfield city councilor. Salary is $80,000, but to get elected, Conrad needs to spend $30,000 for the posters and mail campaign "Conrad White for Change" and "Vote for Honesty and Accountability".

    c) Become the food critic for the *Autumnfield Sun*, which comes with a salary of $20,000 per year.

2.   How many randomly chosen people should be in a room to ensure a 99.9% chance that at least two of them would have the same birthday?

   a)   50.

   b)   127.

   c)   75.

3.   *Pirates of the Caribbean 17*: The legendary pirates Captain Jack Sparrow and Captain Barbossa find a treasure in a cave: two golden nuggets. Jack Sparrow is planning to use them to make two golden teeth to replace those broken by his manager/colleagues/pirates. Barbossa offers Jack only one nugget. What should Jack Sparrow do?

   a)   Accept Captain Barbossa's offer and take one golden nugget.

   b)   Grab both nuggets and run away. In this case there is a 50% chance that captain Barbossa would catch him and keep all the nuggets.

   Pirates of the Caribbean 22: The legendary pirate Captain Jack Sparrow is imprisoned in a dungeon with two other pirates awaiting the hangman's noose the following afternoon. As he plans his escape, he realizes that he can put his two gold teeth to good use. What should he do?

   a)   When his two companions wake, promise them one gold tooth each to aid in his escape (they have not been sentenced to hang). However, once out of the prison he can run away before they can collect their reward. In this case, there is a 50% chance that Jack will lose all of his golden teeth.

   b)   Give a golden tooth to each of the companions.

4.   A Russian spy, Ivan Petroff, infiltrated the White House disguised as a rat exterminator and stole a top-secret document: a list of Washington, DC's approved escort agencies. Three people actually witnessed Ivan Petroff inside the White House. Whose description of the Russian spy is most probable?

    a)   White House bartender Mick Mousy described the exterminator as a big guy in a black suit.

    b)   White House taxi driver Mohamed Toscanini described the exterminator as a big guy in a black suit and sunglasses.

    c)   White House secret service agent Bert Bigneck described the exterminator as a big guy in a black suit and sunglasses, who spoke with Russian accent.

5.   Who is happier (Figure Judgment Test.1)?

    a)   Millionaire Roland Drump: Market value of his Vally's Casino in Las Vegas has dropped over the past five years.

    b)   Engineer John Bored: for the last five years he has been doing the same design of a girder without a raise or promotion.

    c)   Bouncer Jack Fist: over the last five years he has improved his bouncing skill and can now toss a person out of the club with his eyes closed and hopping on one foot. However, his compensation package has not improved.

    d)   Dishwasher James Clean: every year he was promoted to a higher position, including senior dishwasher, lead dishwasher, manager dishwashing, and director of enterprise dishwashing.

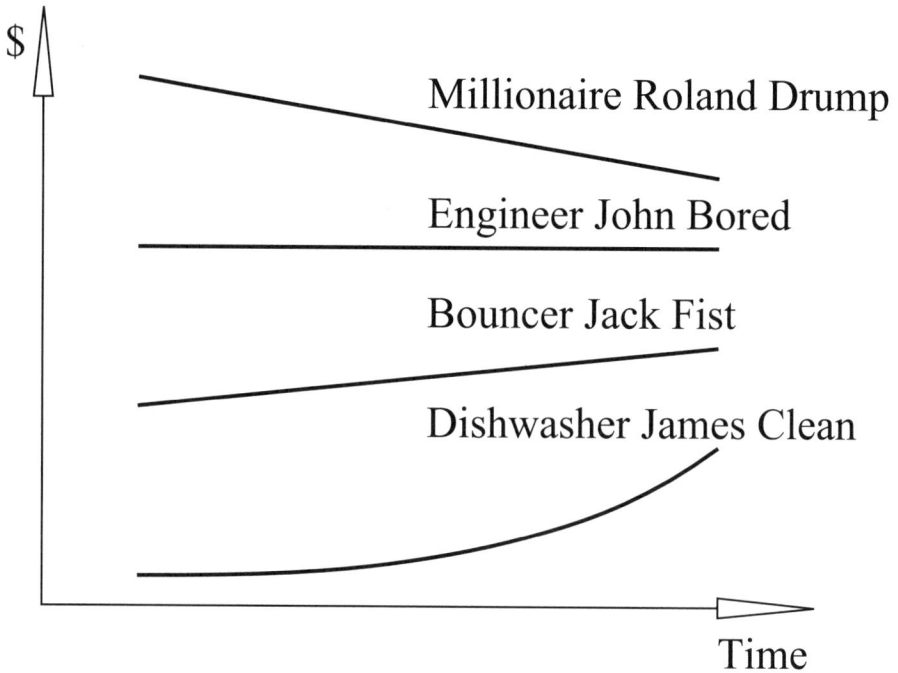

Figure Judgement Test.1 Who is happier?

6. A true story. The Ig Nobel Prizes are a parody of the Nobel Prizes and are given each year for 10 achievements that "first make people laugh, and then make them think". The Ig Nobel 1998 award in Literature was given to Dr. Mara Sidoli of Washington, DC, for her report "Farting as a Defense against Unspeakable Dread", published in the *Journal of Analytical Psychology* (Sidoli 1996). Is farting research:

    a) Stupid.

    b) Irrational and a symptom of psychological problems of the author.

    c) I cannot comment until I read the report.

7. After reading inspirational stories about successful gamblers, you travel to Cesar's Palace casino to play roulette. By 5 p.m. you have

already lost $4,000, by 9 p.m. your losses are $6,000, and by 11 p.m. your losses stand at $8,000. Your wife asks you to stop and threatens to leave you if you continue. What should you do?

a) Stick with it, this losing streak has gone on for so long that it must be about to end. Your chances of hitting a winning streak have increased by 50%. Your wife will be singing a different tune when the good luck starts rolling your way.

b) Your chances to win are always the same. You should listen to your wife and stop.

c) You calculate that your chances of winning have increased by 25% and therefore you will continue, but limit future losses to $2,000.

8. In the movie *Dr. No*, James Bond was, in the following order: almost killed in the car (chance of survival 10%), discovered a tarantula in his bed (chance of survival 10%), almost shot (chance of survival 10%), and almost executed in Dr. No's hideout (chance of survival 10%). What was the overall chance that James Bond survived all of these situations?

a) 10% – equal to eating non-organic cream cheese with 30% trans fat.

b) 1% – equal to drinking tap water in a remote Mexican village.

c) 0.01% – equal to jumping from a plane without a parachute.

9. Hollywood socialite Berlin Sheraton was arrested for driving under the influence. Before her driving and subsequent arrest for driving under the same influence, she had visited the Beverly Hills pub where she:

a) Assaulted a security guard with a lipstick: punishment for this offense is loss of said lipstick.

b) Went to the kitchen and spit in the soup of the day:

punishment for this offense is one year in a minimum security penitentiary.

    c)   Instructed her miniature poodle Jay Y. to attack a barman: punishment for this offense is apprehension of Jay Y.

Police do not know yet about her activities at the bar. Which punishment should most concern Berlin Sheraton if Jay Y. is eight times more important to her than one month in jail, and her favorite lipstick is two times more important to her than Jay Y.?

10.   You are the head coach of new NHL franchise the East Coast Cockroaches. Struggling with a salary cap, a blind goaltender, and a defenseman with ADD, your team lost 20 games in a row. Fortunately, your team won its last two games because of your opponents' team scoring a few times on their own goal. You need to estimate the chance that the Cockroaches will skitter into the playoffs. How will the last two wins affect your estimate?

    a)   Opponents defeating themselves is a growing trend and it should propel the Cockroaches into the playoffs.

    b)   Since you have not really improved the play of your own team, the last two wins should not be considered a trend.

    c)   Your chance to go to the playoffs has increased 10%.

Answers to Judgment Test

1. Correct answer is b. If Conrad robs the bank, he should expect to get $40,000 = $200,000 (payout) × 20% (success rate). As city councilor he would get $50,000 = $80,000 salary – $30,000 (expenses). A food critic career would bring him $20,000. Therefore, the city councilor position would bring him more value.

2. Correct answer is c. This is the so-called birthday paradox. Most of us believe that the number of people in the room would be significantly large (BetterExplained 2010).

3. Correct answer is a. in both *Pirates of the Caribbean 17* and *Pirates of the Caribbean 22*. The expected value cost in all cases will be one golden nugget or one golden tooth. So all cases are identical from the expected value point of view. However, most people would prefer to gamble when they decide about losses and take a sure bet when they decide about gains. So Jack Sparrow would most likely take sure bet 'one tooth from Captain Barbossa', but will gamble to increase the chance that he does not lose teeth. This psychological effect is called "loss aversion". You will learn about it in Chapter 11.

4. Correct answer is a. The more general a description, the more probable the description is.

    Number of people in black suits is greater than

    Number of people in black suits and sunglasses is greater than

    Number of people in black suits, sunglasses, and a Russian accent.

    This problem is related to representativeness heuristic. You may learn more about this heuristic in Chapter 7.

5.   Correct answer is d. As we will learn in Chapter 8, happiness is associated with increments of "units of happiness", which can be wealth, position, title, successful family, etc., but not in absolute number of units. The dishwasher James Clean who is constantly promoted probably is happier than others, even though his net worth is lower. You will learn more about happiness from Chapter 8.

6.   Correct answer is c. You cannot judge rationality without a detailed analysis. In the case of scientific research, you need to read the paper to make this judgment. If something sounds strange and funny, it does not mean that it is irrational. Read about processing information in Chapter 9.

7.   Correct answer is b. Your wife is correct as usual. Many people believe that their chance of winning will increase after a series of losses – the gambler's fallacy. In reality, the chance of winning does not change. You will learn about it in Chapter 11.

8.   Correct answer is c (0.01%). People tend to overestimate the probability of conjunctive events. This is a well-known psychological bias. You will learn about it in Chapter 11.

9.   Correct answer is a. The common denominator would be months in jail. In the case of the lipstick attack, it would be equal to 16 months in jail. Soup-spitting is equal to 12 months, and in the case of Jay Y. it would be 8 months in jail. You will learn the basics about multi-criteria decision-making in Chapter 10.

10. Correct answer is b. People often ignore historical data (long-term average) when they perceive a recent short-term trend. This effect is called ignoring regression to mean. Learn about this effect in Chapter 7.

Now score yourself and see where you fall on Table Answers.1.

Table Answers.1   Some advice based on judgment test

Number of correct answers	Some advice
1–3	Don't worry; most people have difficulties answering these questions. In this book, you will find answers to this and many other questions. Even better, it doesn't appear that your judgment is significantly affected by illusions – as you bought this book. People who are significantly affected by illusions are completely unaware that there might be a problem and tend to spend their money on red cars and cosmetic surgery instead of investing in valuable books such as this.
3–7	You have sound judgment. Tell your boss, maybe you will get a raise (probably not, but it never hurts). Though your boss probably doesn't see any value in your ability to make good choices, you can still improve your decision-making skills by reading this book.
7–10	Your judgment is outstanding and not significantly affected by illusions. You may not need this book at all. Sorry, the authors do not issue refunds or accept returns.

PART I

Why Do Good Managers Make Poor Project Decisions?

1

Mental Errors in
Project Management

It is not uncommon to see good and experienced project managers make poor decisions that lead to issues and eventually project failures. What is the explanation: misjudgment, lack of experience, or do some project managers just run out of luck? People make similar repeatable mental mistakes when they make choices, whether in their personal life or when they manage complex projects. These mental mistakes are a primary source of human error in project management, errors that can eventually lead to project failures.

The Power of Misplaced Perception

Beginning around 1995, a number of large computer companies including Oracle and IBM started a series of ambitious projects. They were trying to develop and market a range of diskless desktop computer devices, which Oracle called a network computer (NC). The idea was quite revolutionary: if computers were mostly used to connect to the Internet, they do not require a very powerful processor, a CD-ROM, or even hard drives. NCs would be much less costly than regular desktop computers were at the time: they could be priced at less than $1,000, a significant cost advantage at the time. Moreover, since the software was installed on a server rather than the NC, the cost to the user to maintain and upgrade it would be substantially reduced. Customers could have a computer that met all of their needs for a fraction of the cost. Despite all of its promise, the idea failed to materialize and NCs were not sold in significant enough quantities (Roth 2009). Why? For this project to succeed at least four conditions had to be met:

1.   The price of regular PC computers must stay way above $1,000 to ensure that NCs would be competitively priced.

2.   The availability of a wide range of compatible software for NCs.

3.   Widespread network availability of network infrastructure sufficient to run NC software.

4.   Widespread acceptance by consumers of the idea of network computing where central control was external: that is, someone else on the server side would be in control of the system and data.

Let's assume that the probability that each condition could be met equals 70%. At first glance, 70% appears to be quite high and chances are promising. But taking a closer look, we can see that there are several conditions that must be met, each of which has a 70% chance. Therefore project success is the product of all of the chances for each condition. It is: 0.7x0.7x0.7x0.7 ≈0.24. So, would you invest millions of dollars on a project with a projected chance of success of only 24%? The makers of the NC most likely faced a similar situation, but went ahead with the project anyway – probably because the executives of these companies were subject to a common mental mistake: they thought that the chance of success was much higher. This mental mistake "overestimating the probability of conjunctive events" is quite common and behind many project failures.

With just this brief example, we can see that organizations are quite capable of repeating apparently poor decisions, but just so you don't think that this is an isolated case, here is another. In the 1980s, the North Korean government was looking to make a bold statement to the outside world that would illustrate the country's industrial and technological power and attract much needed foreign investment. The government's leader came up with a most audacious project – they would construct a building that would be the envy of the rest of the world, a hotel that would not only be the world's largest, but one of the largest buildings of any type in the world, the Ryugyong Hotel (Figure 1.1). This enormous building was planned to reach a height of 1,100 feet, comprising 105 floors. This project represented an investment of a significant percentage of the North Korean GDP (Hagberg 2008) and would become the centerpiece of the North Korean government's efforts to showcase the success of their political and economic system and take some of the shine off of the economic success of their arch enemy South Korea.

Figure 1.1   Ryugyong Hotel in Pyongyang

Source: Joseph Ferris III, Wikipedia.

As fate would have it, the project did not turn out to be the resounding success that the North Korean leadership had envisioned. Huge cost overruns and a host of technical issues ground the project to a halt in 1992, leaving behind a massive derelict concrete shell sitting in the heart of Pyongyang for all to see. Although some work on this hotel resumed in 2009, the construction of the Ryugyong Hotel has had the exact opposite effect that was intended by the Korean leaders. If they had decided instead to build a rocket or a massive ship and the project failed, the reminders of the failure would fade quickly as the evidence would probably have vanished in a huge explosion or lie on the bottom of the ocean hidden from view, as it did in 2012 when a North Korean rocket broke up in flight (Schwarz 2012). When you fail and leave behind a reminder larger than the Great Pyramid of Cheops, everyone is reminded of this every time they look at the city skyline. Can there be a greater humiliation? So while we can understand the motivations behind the decision to start the project, the question – given the great risks – is why the project went ahead in the first place. Were the North Korean leaders unaware of the potential cost? Even given the large amount of risks and uncertainties associated with a project of this size, calculating the costs was not an impossible task.

These stories have at least three things in common:

1.   All managers in these examples had a choice: they could decide not to invest in an unproven computer architecture and they could have chosen not to build an impossibly extravagant skyscraper.

2.   These are not trivial choices.

3.   Eventually, these choices lead to negative consequences, as they were essentially *irrational*.

Why Do We Make Irrational Choices?

What do we mean when we refer to something as irrational? People often use long words to describe simple concepts in the hope that it makes them sound intelligent or hide their true meaning. So they will use words such as irrational when stupid would do just fine. However, *irrationality is not stupidity, it is a contradiction*. It is a contradiction between what we would like to achieve and how we actually choose to achieve it. Why do these contradictions, these irrationalities, occur? Why are good project managers unaware that the decision they have made will not achieve the results they expect? These smart and educated people are capable of making rational choices, but do not do it on a very predictable basis.

Irrationality is a contradiction between what we would like to achieve and how we actually choose to achieve it.

In reality, these decision-makers become subject to mental mistakes. Criss Angel is an illusionist and the star of his own show, *Mindfreak*. In one memorable show, he hypnotized and levitated a young lady in front of stunned spectators on the street in Las Vegas, similar to the picture shown in Figure 1.2.

Figure 1.2   Levitation: classical example of illusion
Source: iStockPhoto.

It was incredible and it was an optical illusion: both the live and TV audience appeared to see the young lady floating in the air; however, according to well-known laws of physics, we know that there must have been some sort of support. It was a very compelling display that tricked our minds into seeing a woman apparently floating in thin air. Here is an interesting phenomenon about all illusions: they require people to make *the same mental errors*. All of the spectators shared the same perception during Criss Angel's illusion: they saw a lady floating in the air. These illusions or errors in perception are common to all people regardless of place of birth, level of compensation, nationality, sexual orientation, political preferences, language and other factors that distinguish us. For example, the mental errors experienced by a CEO and a dishwasher are the same, except the CEO's errors will have much greater impact.

Let's return to Criss Angel and Las Vegas. Here is another optical illusion for you. Take a look at the picture of the Bellagio Hotel and guess how many stories there are (Figure 1.3). Commonly, people estimate that it has about 20 stories, which is precisely what the architect wants us to believe. The actual number is 36.

Figure 1.3   One of the best examples of optical illusion in architecture
Source: Blake, Wikipedia.

The difference between our estimates and reality is caused by a well-designed optical illusion. In addition to optical illusions, there are a large number of other types of standard mental errors that affect our judgment. For example, project managers often use previous similar activities as guidelines when estimating cost for specific activities. Sounds reasonable, basing your estimates on the results of previous similar activities. This appears to be reasonable strategy up to a point, but then they often believe that cost of current activity should be less because of lessons learned, better management, etc. This may be true, but just as often this is a mental mistake: most likely they will make other mistakes and even repeat the previous ones. Here is an actual example. For the past eight years we have been designing and developing our own project management software. Through these years we have had 12 releases and, without a single exception, they were all delayed anywhere from two to six months. Each time we planned a new release date, we suffered from the mental error that we could improve our process and release the software on time even though we were writing books and articles on this very subject at the time.

For Oracle executives, the belief that demand, cost, infrastructure and software availability would be favorable for them was a mental mistake. This mistake led to a contradiction: millions spent on development and marketing of NCs were mostly wasted. The Ryugyong Hotel project is another example of a contradiction: instead of becoming the first building outside New York or Chicago with over 100 floors or the largest hotel building in the world, it could instead have the title: the World's Tallest Incomplete Building.

If critical decisions were not subject to the same mechanisms that lead to mental errors, we would have nothing to worry about. If you are lucky enough to attend one of Criss Angel's shows, see some of his fantastic optical illusions, and appreciate the skills behind the performance, this is nothing but good entertainment. However, if after seeing a *Mindfreak* show you conclude that the law of gravity has been repealed and you start to base some of your decisions on this, you will probably quickly find yourself in trouble, if not severely injured or dead. Unfortunately, the truth is that people often base their decisions using the same mental errors that cause Criss Angel's illusions, which can have disastrous consequences.

Alternatively, it might be fair to ask if mental errors can have unforeseen positive effects on projects. Remember, mental errors are erroneous mental representations of reality. Is it possible to make better choices by perceiving a project differently than it really is? Maybe there is a chance that mental errors could lead to better decisions. However, we strongly believe that critical project decisions must be done based on an analysis of reality rather than mental errors.

Mental Errors in Project Management

We are subjected to mental errors everywhere. Everything we see, listen, touch, taste, and smell can be misinterpreted, and our ability to manage projects is not an exception. In project management, the consequences of irrational choices made due to mental errors are failed projects. Here are a few encyclopedic cases of failed projects (Charette 2005; Hall 2005):

- 1991: an inaccurate structural analysis for the Sleipner North Sea Oil Platform led to the loss of the platform at a cost of $1 billion.

- 1994: the U.S. Federal Aviation Administration canceled a project to upgrade the air traffic control system.

- 1995: an overrun of the development of the Denver airport baggage handling system prevented the airport from opening on time. Fixing the extremely bug-riddled system required an additional 50% of the original budget – nearly $200 million. Confirming that people do not learn from previous mistakes: in 2008 a very similar project at the new terminal at Heathrow airport suffered the same fate; hundreds of flights were cancelled when the baggage system malfunctioned (BBC News 2008).

- 1996–99: several major space exploration projects, including the Mars Polar Lander, Mars Climate Orbiter, and Ariane 5 European Space Launcher, were lost because of various errors.

- 2003: a software bug was determined to be a major contributor in the 2003 Northeast blackout, the worst power system failure in North American history. The failure involved the loss of electrical power to 50 million customers and economic losses estimated at $6 billion.

- 2003–04: Customer relations management at AT&T Wireless because of upgrade problems led to a revenue loss of $100 million.

- 2004: Newly automated supply-chain management system of British food retailer Sainsbury's fails and the company had to hire 3,000 additional clerks. $526 million of investment was written off.

- 2004: Ford Motor Co. abandoned its purchasing system after deployment costing $54.5 million.

- 2005: Hudson Bay Co.'s problem with its inventory management system contributed to a $33.3 million loss.

Researchers who study such projects found that the main underlying reason for these failures is not earthquakes, pine beetle infestations, floods, or other external factors, which are hard to either predict or avoid. Most projects fail because of errors in human judgment, essentially irrational behavior.

Project mental errors are not the only reason for project failures; there is a good measure of incompetence and inexperience lurking in the shadows. But we strongly believe that mental errors are the root causes of many problems. Every year mental errors in project management lead to multi-billion-dollar loses. A 2002 study commissioned by the National Institute of Standards and Technology found that software bugs cost the U.S. economy about $59.5 billion annually, or 0.6% of the gross domestic product (NIST 2002). The same study found that more than a third of that cost (about $22.2 billion) could be eliminated by improved testing. These bugs are not created by nature: animals, volcanoes, and geysers don't develop the software. The problems were caused by the faulty judgment of people.

Figure 1.4 shows a typical road map to project failure.

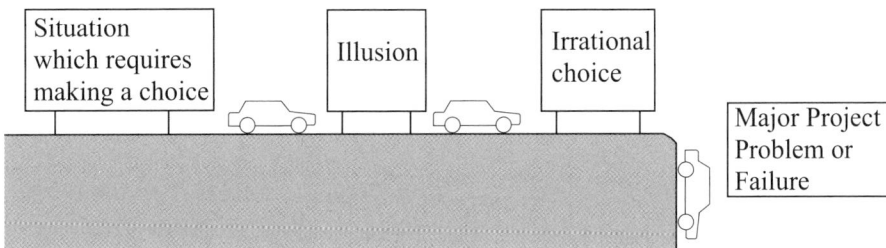

Figure 1.4   Road map to project failure

You have a *situation in a project that will require making some choices*. Here is an example. In 2000, the retailer Kmart Corp., in Troy, Michigan, launched a massive $1.4 billion IT modernization effort aimed at linking its sales, logistics, marketing, and supply systems, to better compete with rival Wal-Mart Corp (Charette 2005). Kmart had many choices regarding the timing and the scale of the project, but decided to pursue a quite ambitious scenario:

1.   **You often have to deal with *mental errors*.** Upper management of Kmart apparently had many other priorities outside of the IT project and was under the illusion that the project would succeed with limited upper management support. This is a very common mental error. Upper management initiates a project with minimum possible resources and then distances itself from the project, somehow hoping that it will succeed by itself.

2.   **These *mental errors* lead to *irrational choices*.** The Kmart IT project had limited budget and manpower. Moreover, the IT project's relationship with the organization's business was not clearly established.

3.   **Irrational choices lead to major project problems or *project failures*.** Eighteen months later Kmart cut back the modernization project, writing off $130 million it had already invested. Four months later Kmart declared bankruptcy.

Mental Errors or Intention?

It is important to distinguish between mental errors and intention. Danish researcher Bent Flyvbjerg and his colleagues reviewed a significant number of large projects (Flyvbjerg 2005). Among them were large transportation projects such as Skytrain in Bangkok, the Channel Tunnel, Los Angeles subway, defense projects such as the Eurofighter military jet, the Nimrod maritime patrol plane, the F/A-22 fighter jet, oil and gas projects such as Sakhalin-1, construction projects such as Hannover Expo 2000, the Scottish parliament building, Ontario's Pickering nuclear plant, and very many others all over the world. Flyvbjerg also talked directly with people who were involved in the politics of megaprojects, such as famous architects Frank Gehry and Kim Utzon. What was common about all these projects is that they were significantly over budget and often took much longer than originally planned.

For example, the Channel Tunnel between the U.K. and France came in 80% over budget for construction.

Flyvbjerg found that project planners often intentionally underestimate costs and overestimate benefits to get their projects approved. He studied data for the past 70 years and found that cost overruns have not decreased over time. This intentional "cooking of the books" is pernicious, not only because it leads to cost overruns, but also to safety, security and other problems.

Intentionally underestimating cost and duration is not the only unethical thing you might do. Here are a few other ideas (just don't tell anybody where you got the idea):

- Although you have spent the last few weeks procrastinating and catching up with your friends on Facebook, tell your boss that you completed the development of the software module two weeks ago, even produce an ugly-looking hand-drawn screen shot as proof of your effort, even though you haven't even started yet.

- Although you have yet to even open the quality assurance manual, create a report that shows the quality control procedure was properly executed and even show that you managed to find several minor defects.

- Although prototype does not actually work yet, tell your project sponsor that the prototype's performance is very close to the specification.

So what is the main reason for human mistakes in project management: honest mental errors or what Flyvbjerg refers to as deception – deliberate errors in project planning, forecasting and execution? Flyvbjerg said that the answer depends on the project (Flyvbjerg 2006). In large projects and megaprojects where political and organizational pressure is very high, deception plays a key role. Whereas in smaller projects, where these pressures are limited, mental errors have a greater role.

But here is one important thought about deception. People who are involved in a deception are mostly motivated by a belief that in the long run it will benefit society (as in the case of many transportation projects); their company (as in the case of Enron or WorldCom); or themselves. In almost all cases, these beliefs are also a mental error. Projects that are approved based on fraudulent forecasts will at the end of the day be a net loss to society. If you create a fake report or tell your manager you are performing tests when in reality you are researching your picks for next week's fantasy football pool, you may be fine in the short term. But this is a mental error, because at the end of the day, you will have to deal with the problems you create.

Why Is Recognizing and Dealing with Mental Errors so Difficult?

All people are subject to illusions. We all make repeatable mental errors, so why all the fuss? Mistakes can be identified and fixed. Perhaps you made a mistake and forgot to turn off the BBQ when you went on vacation. No big deal – some minor fire damage to your neighbors' houses across the street (unfortunately, your house burned to the ground). However, it can be fixed: call your insurance agent, if you happen to have one.

But here is the problem. The mental errors that cause irrational decisions are very cunning. They hide their tracks so well that it is often very hard to determine if there was a mistake and, if there was, what caused it. People who are extremely competent in one area often display poor judgment in others. This explains why successful engineers may not be good project managers, and experienced politicians often cannot properly manage their finances. Thomas Jefferson, the third President of the United States, was a great project manager and was ultimately responsible for the country's finances. At the same time he was deeply in financial debt. During his career in office, Jefferson attempted numerous times to abolish or limit the advance of slavery. At the same time, he owned many slaves and would not free any because of his personal financial difficulties (Sloan 2001). Obviously, if someone like Thomas Jefferson can find themselves in such an irrational situation, anyone can. But why is it so easy to get caught in these irrational situations? Why is irrationality so widespread?

One of the most common sources of such mental errors is people's difficulties in assessing future uncertainties. Wouldn't life be a bit more bearable if we could accurately predict what will occur as a result of our actions? You start smoking: you will die from lung cancer on January 17, 2021 – 24 years earlier than if you hadn't taken up the habit. If you go to the casino today, you will lose $12,798.67, but hold off until tomorrow and you will win $6,589.32. This situation would have some drawbacks as uncertainty is the basis of entire practices, including project management. You would not need to worry that your project would be delayed: it will be completed Friday, June 26, 2015 as scheduled. But it doesn't work that way, does it? You cannot go to a Wal-Mart and buy a crystal ball that provides accurate forecasts of how your project should proceed in the future. Lacking any reliable instruments that provide accurate foresight, people tend to make predictable mistakes when they estimate future risks and then go on to choose a course of action based on these flawed estimates. For example, if you asked people to estimate the risks associated with nuclear and fossil fuel power, most would believe that nuclear power is the more risky option, when in reality, the chance that the burning of fossil fuels will damage your health is far greater.

Here is another issue that leads to many mental errors: choices we make are often based on multiple objectives. Balancing such objectives can be very complex. For example, your project has a tight schedule and a limited budget for expenses. You need to fly from Denver to Phoenix: would you buy a ticket with a stop in Detroit for $200 or a direct flight for $300? (Airlines tell us that it makes economic sense for them to have routes with multiple stops that zigzag across the country, but we are still not convinced that it is rational.) You have to balance two objectives: convenience and time versus price, which may lead to irrationality. In project management everything is very complex: balancing scope, cost, time, quality, and other objectives is fertile ground for potential mental errors.

A final complication is that many mental errors are due to group interactions. For example, during a project meeting, team members may have severe reservations about the project, but do not express them because they are afraid of appearing to be the only hesitant person in the room. Psychologists discovered this phenomenon by researching how the Kennedy Administration's decision to invade Cuba at the Bay of Pigs was made (Janis 2008). Project management is rarely done in isolation. Interactions between different project stakeholders often lead to misunderstandings, communication issues, or incorrect assumptions and expectations. If a group of people is expected to make a decision, it does not necessarily reduce the chance of mental errors; in fact, it leads to other types of mental errors.

SMART TIPS

Regardless of how smart and experienced you are and the position you hold, always remember that your intuition has limitations and may lead to mental errors.

When making project decisions, always ask yourself three questions:

- Has an objective analysis been performed?
- Has all available data been taken into account?
- Did you involve other experts in the decision-making process?

These three questions may prevent you from making mental errors.

2

Analysis vs. Mental Errors

Structured analysis of a situation helps people to overcome the mental errors we discussed in the previous chapter and can improve their judgment. However, more likely than not, prior to making a decision people have not performed any structured analysis, or they misinterpret the results of the analysis. Complicating matters, sometimes the analysis is extremely complex and results may be incorrect. Even if the analysis is performed and is correct, often people do not realize its value. As a result, even now where we have highly trained experts with access to powerful computers, running the most advanced mathematical models, we still bear witness to the outcome of so many poor-quality decisions.

Why Don't People Perform Even a Simple Analysis?

On September 15, 2008, the Lehman Brothers filed for Chapter 11 bankruptcy protection following the massive exodus of most of its clients, drastic losses in its stock, and devaluation of its assets by credit rating agencies. Why did one of the largest and oldest financial firms with $691 billion in assets collapse so rapidly? Superficially, we have been told that their heavy investment in subprime mortgages and associated derivatives were the catalyst that set off the fall of Lehman Brothers. But how did their army of highly educated MBAs and powerful financial models fail to foresee this risk and communicate the threat to the decision-makers at the helm of Lehman Brothers and other related financial institutions to do something about it? Sadly, the truth is that the senior management of Lehman Brothers, particularly CEO Richard Fuld, was well aware of the subprime mortgages problem, having been warned on multiple occasions, but they deliberately chose to ignore these warnings. Moreover, the management carried on a campaign to silence individuals who talked about these risks (McDonald and Robinson 2009). Was this arrogance, ambition, greed, or something else?

Lehman Brothers worked within a framework of government regulations. Government, in this case the Federal Reserve, is supposed to ensure that financial crises like the subprime meltdown should never happen. Did they (the Federal Reserve) see the danger in the type of financial practices associated with subprime mortgages? Apparently yes, but for a long period of time they believed that the problem associated with subprime mortgages would be localized and could not bring down the entire economy (Wessel 2009). Macro-economic analysis is not trivial calculation like simple arithmetic, but surely the Federal Reserve with its significant resources, expertise, and mandate to oversee the economy would be able to foresee the unintended consequences of the financial decisions that were being made by the major U.S. financial institutions. As it turns out they did make mistakes and there are at least three reasons for this.

In complex situations when potential issues are identified, it is generally obvious that an in-depth analysis would help decide on a proper course of action. Low-quality decisions are usually the result of:

1. No or insufficient analysis. This is common in many projects, but not in the case of Lehman Brothers and the Federal Reserve.

2. The analysis is partially or completely incorrect. In our example, the analysis was probably partially correct. The economists in both the Federal Reserve and Lehman Brothers create very complicated mathematical models: however, these models often cannot account for novel or emerging economic processes, in this case the combination of derivatives and the subprime mortgages.

3. Decision-makers amend, ignore, misinterpret, or overwrite results of the analysis. This is what mostly likely happened at Lehman Brothers.

Financial organizations, such as Lehman Brothers, as well as the Federal Reserve are not run by computers (though given recent events it may be not so outrageous an idea); they are run by people who have the discretion on whether or not to accept the recommendations that come from an analysis. As we learned before, people's perception of reality is subject to illusions. People are often under the illusion that analysis is either not necessary or their judgment is better than the direction provided by the analysis. Here is a paradox:

•   We (humanity) consistently fail to make the best decisions given circumstances because we are subject to mental errors.

- To uncover these mental errors and see the correct path, we need to perform some sort of analysis.

- Unfortunately, we often do not perform sufficient analysis because of the mental error that following our own intuition will lead to a better outcome. In other words, we fail to overcome mental errors because we are subject to yet more mental errors.

This leads us to the question, "What types of mental errors make people ignore and misinterpret the results of their analysis?"

Overconfidence

Russian real estate developer Shalva Chigirinsky had extrordinarily ambitious project plans. One of the richest men in Russia with a net worth $2.8 billion in 2008 (Forbes 2008), Chigirinsky had a program to build multiple shopping centers and towers. In particular, Chigirinsky planned to build a huge hotel and entertaiment center just next to the Kremlin in Moscow. The complex was designed by the famous architect Norman Foster. In order to free space for the complex, Chigirinsky's company demolished a 3,200-room hotel. In addition, Chigirinsky wanted to build the tallest skyscraper in Europe, which was to be called the "Russia Tower." Shooting more than 600 meters above ground, the tower would top out at 118 floors (Ermakova 2007). Unfortunately, there is now scant visible evidence of Chigirinsky's ambitious plans. The aftermath of these failed projects is chiefly an empty field across the street from Red Square and an empty lot where Russia Tower was supposed to stand. The unfortunate Chigirinsky found himself as the main protagonist in a series of lengthy court battles. We believe the root cause of Chigirinsky's failure was his overconfience. At the beginning of his career he was a very successful businessman and project manager and, as his businesses grew, his confidence grew and, at some point, his confidence, which was one of his great strengths, became a source of weakness. He became overconfident in his abilities to manage enormous projects.

> *Overconfidence is a psychological bias in which people tend to overestimate the accuracy of their predictions*

Shalva Chigirinsky made at least three mistakes, which are very common in project management:

1.   He was too confident that his business connections would open him any doors and these doors would remain open for a long time. In particular, he had befriended Moscow's mayor Yuri Luzhkov, who was the de facto "czar" of the city. But nothing is forever, relationships could go sour. Yuri Luzhkov was dismissed by the Russian president in 2010.

2.   Chigirinsky was also overconfident about his own resources and money-raising abilities. Overconfidence in quality and quantity of resources, both human and financial, is one of the most common mental errors in project management.

3.   Chigirinsky's overconfidence led him to ignore or understimate different potential risks, particularly the risk of a financial meltdown, which we have already mentioned in this chapter.

Overconfidence in decision-makers is one of the major reasons why analysis is either not performed or the results of analysis are ignored and is one of the most common biases in project management. Let's check whether, as a project manager, you are overconfident or not. For each of the following questions, you must provide a low and high estimate so that you are 90% confident that the correct answer falls between the two estimates. Your challenge is to try to ensure that your estimates are neither too narrow (overconfident) nor too broad (under-confident). Your goal is to try and get at least nine correct answers.

Table 2.1   Test your over confidence

	Question	Low estimate (90% certainty that it will be no less than ...)	High estimate (90% certainty that it will be no higher than ...)
1	How many years did it take to construct the largest Egyptian pyramid – Pyramid of Cheops?		
2	When was the 1st edition of *A Guide to the Project Management Body of Knowledge* (PMBOK Guide) published?		
3	What is the number of floors in the world's tallest building?		
4	What is the length of the Titanic?		
5	How many project management professionals (PMP) were there worldwide in 2010?		

Table 2.1   Test your over confidence (*continued*)

6	What are the proven oil reserves in the U.S. as a percentage of world total proven oil reserves in 2012?		
7	How much did it cost to construct the Pentagon building in Washington, D.C. (Arlington)?		
8	What was the cost of the Apollo space project?		
9	What was the cost of the International Space Station in 2010?		
10	What was the number of passenger cars registered in the U.S. in 2007?		

Psychologists administered a similar test to more than 100 people and found that less than 1% of the respondents got nine or more correct answers. Most people missed four to seven items, which indicated a substantial overconfidence (Russo and Schoemaker 1989). In general, people are confident enough to have a very narrow range for each answer.

Now check your answers and count your incorrect responses:

1. It is believed the Pyramid of Cheops was constructed over a 20-year period (Romer 2007).

2. *A Guide to the Project Management Body of Knowledge* (PMBOK Guide) was first published by the Project Management Institute (PMI) as a white paper in 1983.

3. Burj Khalifa (Dubai) has 163 floors plus 46 maintenance levels in the spire and 2 parking levels in the basement.

4. Length of the Titanic – 882.75 feet, or around 268 meters (Titanic-titanic.com 2010).

5. As of July 31, 2010, there were 393,413 active PMP-certified individuals worldwide (Project Management Institute 2010).

6. The U.S. has 2% of the world's proven oil reserves (British Petroleum 2012).

7. Construction of the Pentagon was completed in approximately 16 months at a total cost of $83 million (Pentagon 2012).

8.   The final cost of the Apollo project was reported to Congress as $25.4 billion in 1973 (House 1974).

9.   The cost of the International Space Station in 2010 was $150 billion (Lafleur 2010).

10.   The number of passenger cars registered in the U.S. in 2007: 135,932,930 (Bureau of Transportation Statistics 2010).

Here are some interesting facts about overconfidence (Plous 1993):

1.   Overconfidence is independent of intelligence. This means that billionaire Shalva Chigirinsky or a bottle-picker, a grade-one drop-out, may both have the same level of overconfidence (Lichtenstain and Fischhoff 1977). The real difference is that if Mr. Chigirinsky has underestimated the required project cost, it may result in losses of millions of dollars; if a bottle-picker overestimates the number of bottles he might find, he may be short a few dollars.

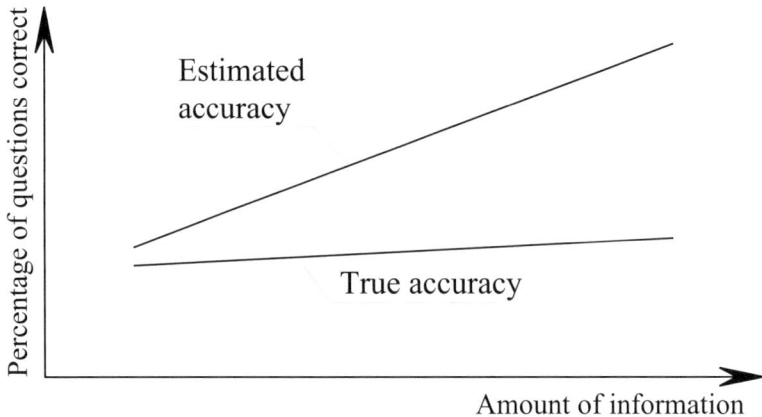

Figure 2.1   More information is not necessary to improve accuracy of judgment, but it may significantly increase level of confidence

2.   More information does not necessarily improve the accuracy of our decisions, but may significantly increase our level of confidence. Practically, this means that the more you learn about a subject, the more confident you will be about your judgment regarding

that subject, but your decision may still be incorrect (Figure 2.1). Managers can have many years of experience in an industry, but can still make poor judgments. This is a very common phenomenon with executives and project managers.

3. Overconfidence is not destiny and can be moderated. If people receive regular feedback regarding the results of their decisions, over time they will exhibit little or no overconfidence. For example, professional bridge players or weather forecasters are less overconfident than project managers who manage different types of projects.

4. If you ask a person to explain why their decisions may be wrong, get them to play devil's advocate to themselves; this will reduce overconfidence (Plous 1993). For example, if Shalva Chigirinsky was asked to explain why he wanted to invest money in such large projects, he might have rethought his decision and rescind his development plans. Answering questions or understanding an opposing perspective might have pushed Chigirinsky and others in his position towards a more balanced and perhaps better analysis of a problem.

Confirmation Bias

Confirmation bias: a tendency to confirm preconceptions or hypotheses, independently of whether or not they are true.

You have arrived in Lisbon, Portugal for a vacation. While walking along the street you hear quite a bit of English being spoken. Because of this, you start to believe that at least half of the Lisbon population speaks English. However, your assessment is incorrect: you simply pay more attention to English-speaking people than the others on the street. This effect is called *selective perception*, or "I see what I want to see."

One manifestation of selective perception is the *confirmation bias*. We cannot know what Lehman Brothers' CEO Richard Fuld was thinking when he was steering his company into a program of risky securities investments that originated in subprime mortgages. But he may already have had the preconceived idea that an investment in subprime mortgage derived securities was the profitable or sound choice, so he might have tended to dismiss evidence that these investments were too risky. In particular, he did not listen to his employees who warned against this strategy. At the same time, he may have put too much weight on evidence to the opposite. For example, because other financial institutions were involved in similar investments, this confirmed his theory.

Confirmation bias can lead to frustrating consequences. For example, confirmation bias is one of the reasons why people are obsessed with conspiracy theories. Did men actually land on the moon? There are those who point to evidence that it did not happen. Examine the picture of Apollo 11 in Figure 2.2. There are no apparent blast craters or any sign of dust scatter in the 16 mm movies of the landing. Conspiracy theorists believe that this confirms their suspicions and the movies and images of lunar landings were staged on a sound studio located in a secret government facility, similar to the manner that the war with Albania in the movie *Wag the Dog* was shot in Hollywood.

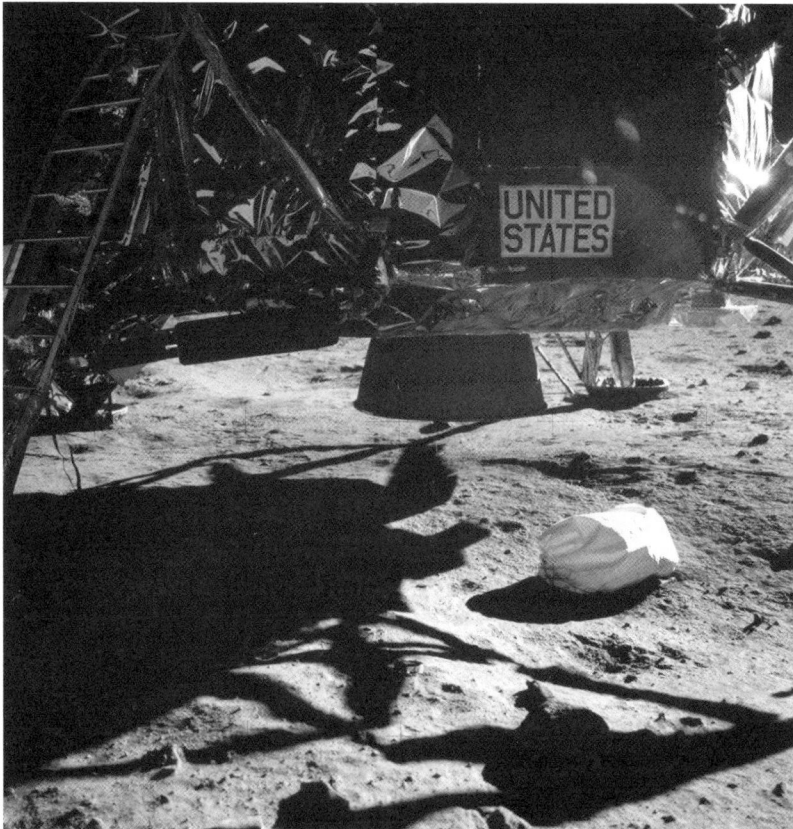

Figure 2.2   Lunar Module Apollo 11 on the moon surface
Source: NASA.

In reality, due to how the lunar module operates, it does not create a blast crater. If you have more such "evidence" and you want to ignore the vast amount of evidence that men actually did walk on the Moon, you are probably a hard-core conspiracy theorist.

Here is an idea: if you manage to derail your project, come up with a conspiracy theory that plays to the preconceptions of your managers. Point to evidence that suggests malfeasance on the part of your competitors, previous management, or poor plan alignment if one of the managers has recently mentioned it. With persistence you should be able to convince management that the issues with the project are not your fault, even if there is a lot of evidence to the contrary.

Confirmation bias is one of the reasons that people do not perform a proper analysis. Why go to all the additional effort to analyze a situation if you already believe that investing in subprime derivatives is the way to go?

Optimism Bias

> Optimism bias is a tendency to be overoptimistic about the outcome of planned actions.

Are you an optimist or pessimist when you are considering the possible consequences of your project plan?

Psychological research shows that most people are overly optimistic about the outcome of planned actions (Armor and Taylor 2002). It is called the *optimism bias* or *planning fallacy*. For example:

- Second-year MBA students overestimated the number of job offers they would receive and their starting salary.

- Most smokers believe they are less at risk of developing smoking-related diseases than others who smoke.

- Most newlyweds in a U.S. study expected their marriage to last a lifetime, despite being aware of the divorce statistics.

In project management, optimism bias affects estimations of many kinds. For example, professional cost estimators consistently underestimate costs of their projects. Here is another problem. Even as a project nears a deadline and cannot be realistically completed on time, optimism bias pushes the manager to report that the project will be completed as planned.

We are not implying that optimism is bad. Most of mankind's greatest achievements were entirely dependent upon someone's abundant optimism that they could overcome insurmountable odds. Without optimism, there would be no persistence. Who would risk starting a new business or get married without it?

At the same time, optimism bias can lead to major blunders, much in the same manner that overconfidence or confirmation bias can lead to a lack of analysis. Optimism bias also manifests itself when we underestimate project cost, duration, and available resources. Perhaps Richard Fuld was overly optimistic about the outcome of investments in subprime mortgage backed securities.

Optimism bias is a mental error which is very hard to overcome. For example, each time we go on vacation we spend significantly more than we plan, regardless of whether we know of this bias or not.

Analysis Is Not Trivial

What causes more greenhouse gases: using paper towels or hand dryers? It is extremely difficult to tell conclusively, though some have tried. What are all the factors that we would have to take into account? Greenhouse gases are emitted during the production of paper, electricity, and the hand dryer itself. How much depends on different conditions: there are different types of paper and hand dryers, electricity can be produced from different sources, and human hands come in many different sizes. How were the towels or dryers transported to their current location? We have just barely scratched the surface and already it has become quite complex.

Since analysis can be very complex, it creates an opportunity for intentional or unintentional misinterpretation. Here is another example. The Canadian company TransCanada is planning to build the Keystone Pipeline System from Alberta to Oklahoma and then to Texas to bring Canadian oil to U.S. refineries (TransCanada 2012). The cost of the project is estimated to be approximately US$7 billion. Environmentalists strongly opposed this project because of two main reasons. First, environmental groups are trying to curtail further development of Canadian oil sands, which they consider particularly "dirty" as these projects have a higher level of greenhouse gas emissions for each unit of energy produced. Second, the pipeline is supposed to cross the environmentally sensitive Sandhills region and huge Ogallala Aquifer, the prime source of drinking and irrigation water for Nebraska and surrounding states. Environmentalists organized massive protests against the project, including staging a demonstration near the White House. Eventually in 2011, the U.S. government decided to postpone the project to select a better route, even though its own regulatory authority had approved the original route. Is this project really bad for the environment? Potentially, yes. There are always risks that a pipeline can leak oil into the aquifer. Oil spills from pipelines happen on a regular basis in the U.S. and Canada. On the other hand, TransCanada has pointed out that there are currently 200,000 miles (320,000 km) of pipelines in the U.S. and the Keystone pipeline is supposes to be the most technologically advanced pipeline ever. Moreover, if a pipeline uses a longer route, the chance of the leak or spill would increase. In the absence of an oil pipeline, producers will use alternate means to ship their oil, which will increase the risk of environmental damage as pipelines are significantly less risky than any of the alternatives. So it looks like efforts by environmentalists may be counterproductive and lead to more environmental problems. The question is, what is the truth? Who is right: the environmentalists or the oil industry? Without undertaking a very complex analysis, people on both sides will make multiple mental errors. Environmentalists tend to rely on vivid descriptions of potential leaks often told by celebrity spokespeople who do not have access to any reliable data. On the other side, we have extremely confident (overconfident) industry experts who are convinced that the planned safety measures will be sufficient. Therefore, you hear all sorts of different assessments that are often contradictory even though they all seem to be coming from reputable sources. The main problem is that even very advanced analysis of a project can give misleading results. That is why so many people, including perhaps Richard Fuld, do not believe it is worth the effort.

What Is the Value of the Analysis?

Kutsch and Hall researched why project managers rarely use risk management and risk analysis in IT projects (Kutsch and Hall 2009). They interviewed a number of project managers and received feedback like this:

- We don't have the time.

- Upper management did not ask for it.

- It is unnecessary or not important.

Project managers have a point: any analysis costs money. Does it make sense to spend this money and what value will the analysis bring? In fact, in many cases intuitive thinking is quite sufficient for making good decisions.

Daniel Kahneman researched intuitive thinking and its limitations (what he called system one) and analytical thinking (what he called system two) (Kahneman 2011). System one produces mental mistakes; system two is supposed to provide more accurate answers. It is important to know that both systems live together side by side within an individual's mind. So at the very least, a preliminary analysis can be conducted without additional cost by just engaging your own system two.

Measuring the value of decision analysis versus intuitive thinking is not very trivial and only limited research has been done on the subject. However, research performed in a few selected companies and projects demonstrate that decision analysis actually provides significant benefits. Clemen and Kwit (2001) studied the use of decision analysis at the Eastman Kodak company. They analyzed the decision-making in 178 projects that were carried out over a period of 10 years. Clemen and Kwit were trying to determine an incremental dollar value generated by decision analysis. In most cases it was hard to measure the actual value added to Eastman Kodak's business, but their estimate was that for all the projects combined, decision analysis added more than $1 billion in value. Clemen and Kwit concluded that even though it was hard to measure value in specific projects, decision analysis brought substantial value to the company.

In many cases, especially those that deal primarily with human emotions or behavior, such as crime prevention or politics, or health care, detailed analysis may not bring better results. However, when dealing with information where it is possible to get objective measures, such as in finance or project management, analysis can significantly improve the quality of decisions. The issue is that in most cases people could not assess the value of the analysis before it is done.

SMART TIPS
- To overcome confirmation bias be honest about your motives and always seek the advice of others. Find a devil's advocate to understand an opposing view and highlight weaknesses in your project plans.
- Always remember that you intuitively tend to be overoptimistic: when you plan your project, always ask "What else can happen?"
- Projects are more complex than simply multiplying 2x2 and cannot be managed solely using intuition. Always resist the temptation to make project decisions without first applying a reasonable level of analysis.

3

Choice Engineering

As we have shown, people often make poor choices because of mental errors. At the same time, they don't perform any analysis that would improve their decisions because of other mental errors to which they are subject. Is there a solution to this problem? Establishing effective processes is always considered a good way to improve project management. For example, if a project manager follows mandatory guidelines for time, scope, cost, risk management and other knowledge areas, this should improve the quality of the decisions made during the execution of the project and reduce the chance of failure. But such processes are hard to implement, often expensive, and followed grudgingly (if at all) by some team members once they have been introduced. In many cases, especially for smaller projects, it would be more beneficial to create an environment within which people are encouraged on their own volition to make better choices, rather than mandate these choices. This is called *choice engineering.*

The Processes vs. Mental Errors

The number of doctors per capita in Russia is significantly higher than in the U.S.: 4.25 per 1,000 people vs. 2.3 per 1,000 people based on 2002–03 data (Nationmaster 2010). In most cases, Russian doctors are as qualified as physicians in Western Europe and North America. At the same time, the quality of health services in Russia is significantly lower than in these countries. There are many reasons to explain this difference: relative lack of equipment and medicine is certainly a major factor. But perhaps more fundamentally is the situation where standard medical processes are either absent or poorly implemented. For example, after cleaning a floor, a nurse may go directly to assist with the delivery of a baby without first washing her hands, or a doctor may perform surgery after a night of heavy drinking. The fundamental reason for these problems, as we have already learned, is mental errors. The doctor is under the illusion that he can successfully remove an appendix despite his hangover. Because of mental errors, the doctor makes a poor decision.

There are processes that could mitigate this and other similar situations. For our example, a campaign could be conducted to educate surgeons that, contrary to their own beliefs, drinking a bottle of vodka prior to performing surgery will not improve their performance, and is not only detrimental to their health, but that of their patients. Hospitals could routinely institute sobriety checks, or require the surgery team to undergo a quick breathalyzer test before surgeries are performed. A process could be put in place to contact replacement surgeons if they are required and so on.

The Project Management Institute's *A Guide to the Project Management Body of Knowledge* (PMBOK® Guide) (Project Management Institute 2013) is an accumulation of the experience of hundreds of project managers and defines the most important project management processes. If these processes are followed, it should significantly improve the performance of the organization. The problem is that implementing and maintaining these processes is hard work.

For example, you are managing a project that will establish an international counterfeit goods production and distribution organization. Such a project may have many risks, including potential arrest by various law enforcement agencies, inaccurate counterfeit Rolex watches, continuously breaking handles on fake Louis Vuitton bags, and fake Viagra which creates nothing but diarrhea. Because of the risky nature of this project, you would like to set up a risk management process. Here is what you need to do:

1. Assign somebody in your organization or hire a consultant to tailor a risk management process for your counterfeiting operation.

2. Find and evaluate tools that can perform risk analysis and management. Then purchase the software and roll it out to your organization. Your IT department will be unhappy as they will now have the added burden of supporting said software (IT is never happy about anything). You need to ensure that the software can communicate with other software used in your business, for example your counterfeit inventory management system, but good luck. Software applications resist most attempts to communicate with each other despite claims of "seamless integration."

3. Your workers will require training both to use the software and follow the new process. This will be quite difficult as your counterfeit business has gone global – goods produced in China,

packaged in Malaysia, shipped from Brazil, and sold in the U.S. Everybody speaks a different language.

4. You then need to put a review or auditing system in place to ensure that the risk management system is being used properly. You need to ensure that all required fields are consistently defined. For example, the probability of the risk that the "Counterfeit Giorgio Armani dress will not be completely destroyed after first wash" equals 1%, the impact is "full loss of the item," and the cost of risk is $0.01 (as the customer will never be able to track down the seller, let alone you, the manufacturer). The risk management strategy is "Accept." Done many times, this represents a lot of information that your employees must enter and track. There is a good chance that they will look for shortcuts or ignore the process altogether. As a further complication, you must take into account that your organization may be running several other processes and systems.

Most processes are strictly defined. People *must* perform their task in a certain order: enter risks with their properties, analyze risks, define risk management plan, update risk status, convert risks to issues, close risks, etc. All of these steps are mandatory: if a step is not completed, the whole process can grind to a halt or provide misleading information. If the most important risk – "Merchandise is confiscated" – is not entered into the system, the process will fail. It would be like publishing a dictionary but not including several commonly used words. Since it would be unclear how many words were missing, the comprehensiveness and usefulness of the dictionary comes into question. Where such systems or processes are unquestionably useful is in situations where things are explicitly banned, as in airline security. While we may question the efficacy of banning certain things from airline flights, having strict processes to ensure that banned products or objects do not make it onto the plane is an effective way of meeting this goal.

So currently you are looking at spending considerable time and resources on a risk management system, but it is apparent that any savings you may gain from it may be less than what you must spend to implement and maintain it. If your business is large and complex, it will probably make financial sense to go ahead with the system as there is a good chance that it will save you money. But if your counterfeit project is relatively small, you only produce and sell counterfeit Gucci shoes and the only risks you have are "broken heel" (pre-sale of course) and "competition from counterfeit Gucci shoes". What if you don't need to explicitly ban something?

What Is Choice Engineering?

Minnesota tax officials conducted the following experiment. Groups of taxpayers were given four kinds of information:

Group 1: Were told that their taxes will go towards paying for services that they generally approved of: education, policing, etc.

Group 2: Were threatened with punishment for non-compliance with the tax system.

Group 3: Were provided information on how they could find assistance for filling out their tax forms.

Group 4: Were told that 90% of Minnesotans had already properly completed their tax returns.

So which group was most likely to submit a correct tax return on time? If you answered Group 4, you are correct. As it turned out, the other interventions had little or no impact on tax compliance. This study points out that people are more likely to follow certain rules if they believe that other people are following them as well. Providing the information that most people were complying with the tax system essentially created an environment in which people made better choices. Without instituting a strict process or threatening penalties, people were encouraged to make good choices themselves; the process helped to steer them towards a better choice, but without restructuring or eliminating their freedom of choice. The original idea was suggested by Richard H. Thaler and Cass R. Sunstein (Thaler and Sunstein 2007). They called this "choice architecture;" their choice of a title was most likely due to the focus of their work – how people make decisions in regards to health and wealth. In project management, we refer to the same concept as "choice engineering."

> Choice engineering is a creating of processes or environment in which people would be steered towards making better choices rather than mandating these choices.

One of the simplest examples of choice engineering is a checklist. Commonly, when you need to fill out a number of related forms, you are also given a checklist that allows you to check that you have filled out and included all of the required forms. You can use the form or ignore it at your own peril, but most of us will choose to refer to it. Alternatively, you could choose just to penalize people who fail to complete the forms properly; you may get compliance, but it would be short lived and resentfully given. It is much more effective to provide a simple checklist.

As for our counterfeiting project, if your organization is relatively small and uncomplicated, you might instead provide a simple list of common risks rather than a comprehensive risk management system. There will still be a process, but with much less strict rules. For example, this risk list will appear each time shipment information is entered into the computer system, which will encourage your employees to think about the risks and hopefully address them on a regular basis. What is most important is you *don't mandate* the use of this risk list. You create an environment in which people can use the risk list in an easy and relatively unobtrusive manner by applying a few simple rules.

Policing vs. Choice Engineering?

Policing is an alternative to choice engineering and refers to mandating choices or certain analysis procedures.

As with any other organizations, the intelligence community is also occasionally involved in complex projects which need proper management. On September 6, 1976, the Russian fighter pilot Victor Belenko defected to Japan in his Mig-25 fighter plane (Barron 1983). He took off from a military airstrip in the Russian Far East, landed at a civilian airport in Japan and instantly requested to be transferred to U.S. authorities. The airplane's systems and weapons, which were quite advanced, were reviewed by U.S. authorities. The airplane itself was later returned to the Soviet Union. A few years after Belenko's defection, Russian newspapers carried the news that Belenko had been killed in a car accident. The subtext of this article was that the KGB had had a hand in the accident. In reality, Belenko is still alive and well. Rumors about KGB agents assassinating political opponents were greatly exaggerated by Hollywood. To discourage people in the Soviet Union from defecting, the KGB had engaged in choice engineering. Killing a dissident outside of the Soviet Union is an expensive and complicated endeavor; it is far easier just to plant a story and let people make their own choices. Given the financial problems the Soviet Union was facing, can you imagine how much it would cost for the KGB to send an agent to the U.S., pay for his travel, accommodation, drinks, and various payments involved in organizing a traffic accident? Then multiply it by the number of all the defectors who had fallen into disfavor with the regime and this would entail a significant portion of the KGB budget. Essentially, the KGB had two alternatives: *policing* (assassination) or choice engineering. Of the two, the latter is by far the easiest and cheapest route.

As we learned in the previous chapters, people make bad choices because they are affected by certain mental errors and are unable to correctly analyze situations. Both policing and choice engineering will help people make better choices (Figure 3.1). However, policing entails a significant restriction in choices and it is the freedom of choice that is the main lubricant in society. Without freedom of choice, projects, technology, and society would gradually grind to a halt. Therefore, it is in our best interests to provide a framework that allows freedom of choice while encouraging choices that are in their best interests.

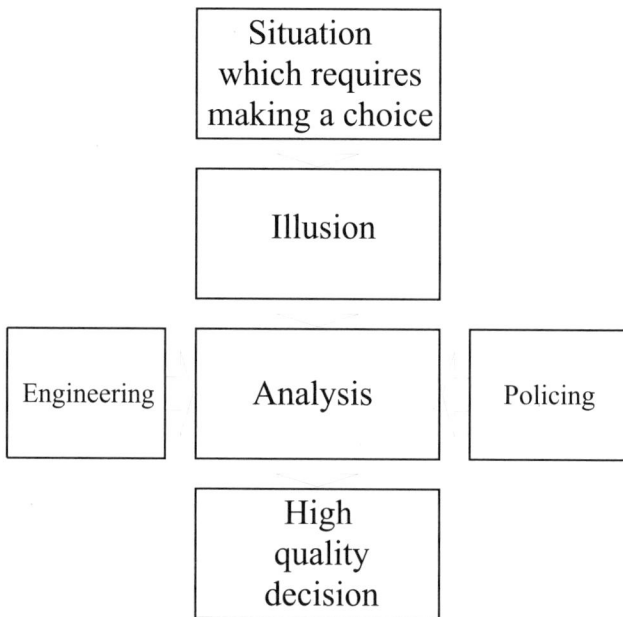

Figure 3.1   **Choice engineering and policing helps people to perform better analysis**

For example, how can we minimize smoking? The government could try prohibition, but as experience has shown, this tends to foster black markets and criminal enterprises. In this example, policing will be a very unproductive approach and most people understand this. Instead, governments and health organizations have turned to choice engineering. Choice engineering entails limiting smoking to specific areas, restricting tobacco advertising, increasing the price of tobacco products, etc. People can still choose to smoke, but the cumulative effect is an environment that is not very supportive for smoking. Most important in choice engineering is that it must be structured around human psychology. For example, messages that are conveyed graphically have a greater effect on people's choices than verbal messages. Graphic messages are used extensively in Canada's anti-tobacco campaign. All cigarette packs include very graphic images of diseases caused by smoking – cancerous lungs, ulcerous sores, etc. Not pretty, but effective. Some other ways to fight tobacco addictions happen to be less effective because of psychological reasons. Therefore, choice engineering must be founded on good knowledge and understanding of human decision-making.

Here is another advantage of choice engineering. The more rules we create, the more opportunities there are to break these rules. Since there are very few rules in choice engineering there is a greater chance that these rules will be followed.

When Policing Is Necessary

Recall from Chapter 1 the discussion on mental errors and intentions. In large projects, estimators and managers often consciously or unconsciously provide false estimates and other incorrect information to get projects approved or to advance some other agenda. In these situations (large and complex), it is important to set up a clear set of rules which *must* be followed.

For example, NASA and other national space agencies have defined multiple processes for risk management for the International Space Station. Obviously these processes are comprehensive and have vigorous controlling procedures. One of these processes is specifically designed for protecting the space station against meteoroids and other orbiting debris. A document of more than 60 pages prepared by a dedicated committee outlines in detail how to mitigate the threat (collision warning and shielding), what to do if an impact has occurred, and most importantly, who is responsible for what (Committee

1997). For projects like the International Space Station, policing is critical to its success.

In each project there is space for policing and choice engineering (Figure 3.2). In large projects, where the role of deception plays a significant role in poor decisions, policing should play a major role as it would be difficult to eliminate deception by choice engineering. At the same time, in smaller projects the role of mental errors in creating bad choices is much more prevalent and choice engineering is an effective tool to drive people towards better choices. Prior to 2008, most governments failed to regulate some of the more complex activities associated with securities, particularly derivatives and their trading. Regulators relied mostly on choice engineering: they thought that the market would provide the corrective mechanisms to punish poor choices. After the financial crisis of 2008–09, more rules were introduced and more rules are still being considered: the ratio of policing vs. choice engineering in this area is continuously shifting towards policing. At the same time, a significant amount of freedom of choice for financial managers still remains. Completely removing the freedom of choice would be the equivalent of moving to a socialist or centrally managed economy.

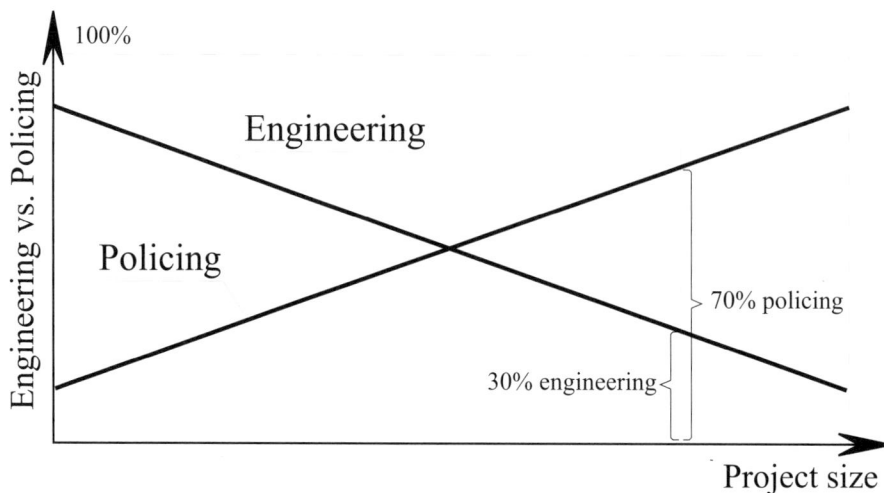

Figure 3.2   Policing vs. choice engineering

Table 3.1 illustrates the difference between policing and choice engineering.

Table 3.1   Comparing policing and choice engineering

		Policing	Choice Engineering
1	Freedom of choice	Significantly restricted.	Much less restricted.
2	Cost of establishing and running	Expensive.	Relatively inexpensive.
3	Problems with establishing and running the process	Easier to define by describing rules and guidelines. Difficult to maintain because compliance must be constantly monitored.	Requires knowledge and understanding of human psychology. Choice engineering is harder to define, but easier to control.
4	Mitigating effects of unintentional mental errors and deception (intentional errors)	Most effective in mitigating deception.	Most effective in mitigating negative effect of mental errors.
5	Where to use	Large projects and certain areas of all projects, where strict processes are necessary, e.g. safety and security.	Any projects where poor-quality decisions are possible due to mental errors.

A Few Ideas Behind Choice Engineering

Here are a few simple things you can do in your project to establish choice engineering.

CHECKLISTS AND TEMPLATES

These are the most simple tools for choice engineering. No complicated procedures, just checking a few checkboxes to ensure that they have not forgotten anything. If you want people to follow a risk management process, don't ask them to memorize Chapter 11 of the PMBOK® Guide (Project Management Institute 2013). Just provide a risk identification template with a few predefined standard risks. Limit paperwork. A rule of thumb is as much as needed, as little as required.

FULL DISCLOSURE

Perhaps you have been asked to participate in the development of a new software product that is estimated to take one year to commercialize. You have a few questions. Who will buy it? How much will it be sold for? How will potential clients use it and what are the proposed benefits? You discover no one on the development team knows much about it. Management probably know the answers, but have not passed that information onto the development team, assuming that they don't need to know this information; it is not critical to the performance of their job. One final question: would you take on this project, would you enjoy working in this environment? This is critical; without this information, a key motivational factor is missing – why are we doing this project, what value to our clients does it represent? Without this essential knowledge, you might as well be digging one hole to fill another. The thought is not inspiring. Therefore, it is incumbent upon management to tell or "disclose" to their project team as much information as possible. Further, they should always take steps to ensure that this information reaches and is understood by the project team. Often organizations simply dump information onto the company website on some obscure URL and then claim that everything has been provided. Full disclosure is a type of choice engineering that addresses many problems with the projects, particularly the disengagement of project team members, who do not feel any ownership in the end product and just work from 8 to 5. Full disclosure pushes people toward better choices without enforcing them.

AUDITING AND INDIRECT CONTROL

Choice engineering does not mean that there are no processes nor any control. What is distinct about choice engineering is that for many projects there is no practical or cost-effective way to implement comprehensive controls on project management procedures. Instead, choice engineering relies on audits and indirect control of project management processes. At issue is if people manage to make irrational choices, e.g. take unnecessary risk and get away with it, they may continue this behavior in the future. Audits can prevent this effect. Audits and indirect controls performed on a regular basis will help to ensure that people continue to make rational choices. For example, as a project manager you need to ensure that your team follows the project plan. Regardless of whether you use policing or choice engineering, following the project plan is necessary. You may ask your team members to enter their daily project-related activities into a sort of project management system. This would be policing and may be perceived as being a bit heavy-handed. Alternatively, you can schedule regular project status meetings in an informal environment where everybody would briefly report on their recent activities and progress. These meetings would encourage people to think of their answers and as a result they will try to align their activities with the project plan. This occurs not because there is an explicit procedure to stick to the project plan, but because there is an environment which motivates people towards performing congruently with the project plan.

COMPETITION

Competition between different organizations helps to create better products. Competition between different project teams and even between different groups of people within a project team will foster an environment that pushes people to do more analysis, which leads to better choices, and eventually find better solutions. Here is a true story. Two crews constructed two parallel subway tunnels in Minsk, the capital of Belarus. They started at the same time and both tunnels were identical. After a month or two, it was discovered that one crew was constructing the tunnel faster than the other. The technology and machines were the same, the crews had similar qualifications and experience, and they were using the same materials. If only one tunnel had been constructed, nobody would probably bother with trying to perform any detailed analysis of productivity. But in this case the question was raised: Why? After some investigation, it was determined that the core reason for the difference in construction speed was not any objective factors, but poor project management and particularly human management practices used in one of the crews.

MAKE PROCESS A HABIT

At one time the Greyhound Bus Line safety record was not perfect: the number of accidents was higher than its competitors. To fix this problem, Greyhound introduced very strict safety procedures. It was very hard and costly to establish them, follow them, and monitor them. For example, all employees, including office administrators, every week had to submit a fixed number of safety observations or warnings into the corporate risk management system. Naturally, people complained, as hazardous situations were relatively infrequent – and almost non-existent for office workers. To meet quotas, people started to enter frivolous entries into the system: one wrote that if a person enters a kitchen too quickly or without warning, someone might accidentally hit them by opening the refrigerator door. Another entry made notice of the hazard of people colliding with one another when turning the corner in the office corridor. After a month or two, management dropped the requirement to submit these entries and it became voluntary. The upside of this was that people were now conditioned that if a real hazardous situation presented itself, they could use the system to immediately report it. In this case, a small "policing" exercise helped to create a habit: policing transformed to choice engineering.

EDUCATION

Project management education and training with a focus on decision analysis and human psychology is an important choice engineering tool. For example, you decided to cheat on your taxes (just a little bit). The reason why you think that you will be fine is that you do not know how many people have actually been caught. This is a very common mental error in which people make choices based on incorrect assumptions or incomplete information. Instead of checking statistics regarding the rate that tax evaders are discovered, you instead rely on your gut feelings or intuition. In reality, tax authorities have quite a good record at discovering tax evaders, including small ones. If you learn about different types of mental errors, it will help to minimize the chance that you will be a subject of these mental errors.

In the next part of this book you will learn about common psychological errors and pitfalls, and what to do about them.

SMART TIPS
- When managing projects, try to create environments in which people will make rational choices: choice engineering. It should be cheaper, faster, and often more effective than creating and implementing strict managerial processes (policing).
- In all projects there is space for both policing and choice engineering.
- Examples of choice engineering methods are: using checklists, providing comprehensive information to the project team, auditing and indirect control, embracing competition, trying to make processes a habit, and engaging in project management education and training.

PART II

Travel Inside a Project Manager's Mind

4

Memory and
Project Mental Errors

In this book, we discuss a few psychological concepts related to decision-making in project management: memory, emotions, heuristics and biases, mental traps, and happiness. A better understanding of ourselves should translate to a better understanding of others and allow us to improve how we manage projects. A lot of the mental mistakes we are prone to in project management are related to memory. Often, we cannot properly assess events because we have forgotten similar events that occurred in our past. In this chapter, we will explore how certain features of our memory can affect project management and how we can improve our memory and hopefully improve our project management.

Memory Errors in Project Management

The West Gate Bridge is a steel box girder cable-stayed bridge in Melbourne, Australia. The total length of the bridge is 2,582.6 meters (8,473.1 feet). The West Gate Bridge carries five lanes of motor vehicle traffic in each direction.

On October 15, 1970, during construction, the 112-meter (367.5 foot) 2,000-ton span plummeted into the Yarra River. Thirty-five construction workers were killed, most of whom were having lunch beneath the bridge. The ensuing investigation concluded that the bridge collapsed because of errors in structural design and construction. On the day of the collapse, construction workers were trying to connect two half-girders, which were not fully vertically aligned. Engineers proposed to load higher half-girders with 10 concrete blocks weighing 8 tons each. This extra weight caused the span to buckle and ultimately led to the collapse (Hitchings 1979). Eventually the damage was repaired and the bridge currently serves as a vital link between the city center and its suburbs (Figure 4.1).

Figure 4.1   West Gate Bridge, Melbourne, Australia
Source: iStockPhoto.

Why did the engineers decide to add the additional weight to the bridge during construction? Because they took for granted that the structure would handle the additional weight and no analysis of the proposed solution was necessary. The root cause of such failures of judgment is usually attributed to ignorance, insufficient knowledge, lack of experience, or miscommunication between the different engineering and construction teams. But it is very important to remember that behind each such failure there are a number of fundamental psychological problems, biases, and mental errors. We believe that one of the fundamental reasons behind this construction mistake, as well as many others, was memory errors. Engineers and project managers often don't remember to analyze certain risks or forget to perform necessary analysis. In our example, it is hard to believe that people did not to consider that the extra weight could destroy the structure: every child that has ever played with Lego understands this concept. But professionals must "remember" that under certain conditions, such as adding weight, they must perform the analysis. It is a very basic part of engineering education.

An important thing about memory errors is that they are often accompanied by other mental mistakes. We cannot say that the bridge specifically failed because the bridge's engineers forgot to perform an analysis. Most likely it was a combination of memory mistakes, optimism bias, overconfidence, and other mental mistakes. But memory error was one of original issues leading to other biases; therefore, it is so important to understand and mitigate memory errors.

Let's say you forgot where you put your glasses. In the best case scenario is that you eventually find them, or in the worst case you have to buy another pair – no big tragedy. If a project manager forgets about a certain risk and manages the project without taking it into account, there can be dramatic consequences. In project management most memory mistakes are related to risk identification, because certain risks or their potential impacts are easy to forget. Mistakes of this type occur when organizations do not have a process for risk management and analysis.

What Is a Memory?

Sometimes people think about memory as a tank of water. We fill the tank with information; once it is filled, to add new information, we need to empty it a bit and then add new information. The tank may have a leak – we may forget something. In reality, this model is incorrect: our memory is not a simple storage tank. It is much, much more complex. Here are the three most important concepts about memory:

1.   Memories are generated when information is recorded. The quality and substance of the memory depends on several factors, including the situation, environment, and other experiences that occurred during the time when the memory was formed. Daniel Gilbert (Gilbert 2006) demonstrated it using the following example. Take a look at the cards shown in Figure 4.2. Pick one card and remember it. In a few pages we will come back to this example.

Figure 4.2   Pick one card
Source: iStockPhoto.

2.   Different pieces of information are not stored as discrete units in our brains. We do not simply memorize different pieces of information; we construct and memorize general scenarios (Roediger and McDermott 1995). Let's demonstrate it. Here is a list of words: *Quality Control, Project Execution, Risk Management, Project Time Control, Procurement Management, Project Scope, Meeting with Stakeholders, Project Sponsor, Gantt Chart, Project Cost Analysis, Agile Method, Human Resources Management, Critical Chain.*

Now, without looking at the list, guess which phrases were not in there: *Project Sponsor, Project Management, Drunk Driving,* and *Project Cost Analysis?* One correct answer is *Drunk Driving.* However, there is another correct answer: *Project Management.* Because all the words in the list were closely related to project management, your brain processed and saved them together. Under normal circumstances, it is a very efficient way to memorize things. But in this case your brain was misled.

3.   Memories are reconstructed when we recall information. This information may include memories of the original experience blended with other information. Try it yourself (Myers 2007). Close your eyes and try to recall a pleasurable situation you experienced in the past. So what do you see? Most likely you will see an image of yourself. But if you can see yourself, it is not an original scene; it is a reconstructed scene based on your original experience.

All of these effects make our memory quite unreliable. The result is that when we try to compare different memories with actual events, we may be subject to mental errors that can lead to wrong decisions. For example, when you try to identify project risks, you may remember risk associated with one particular project or type of project because this information is stored together. You may not remember risks from other projects even if these risks can be potentially applicable to your current project.

Reconstructive Memory

The way memories are recorded and recalled is very dependent on context. Psychologists conducted the following experiment (Loftus and Palmer 1974). They showed students different movie clips that depicted traffic accidents. Then they asked one-fifth of the students "About how fast were the cars going when they contacted each other?" An equal number of students were asked the same question, except "contacted" was changed to "hit," "bumped," "collided," or "smashed." The result was that the average speed estimate by students who were asked the question with the word "smashed" was 9 miles per hour faster than by students who were asked the question with the word "contacted" (40.8 miles/hour vs. 31.8 miles/hour).

The week after watching these movies, the psychologists asked students if they remembered broken glass when the cars "smashed" or "hit" each other. If students were asked the question with the word "smashed," they were the most likely to recall some broken glass, although in the movies there was none. This example shows how we reconstruct previous experiences based on memory and other information.

The human memory works in such a way that while recollections may appear quite realistic and tangible, various details may have been gleaned from other sources of information, especially if there is a significant period of time between the event and the attempts to recall it. This makes interpretation of past events very difficult. Police investigators, lawyers, and judges know about this effect, because sometimes it is difficult to understand what was real and what was a product of the witness's imagination.

This effect has important implications in project management. Project managers' experiences will be reconstructed most likely in the context of the most recent project he or she was working on.

How Memories Are Created

Now let's go back to our card example. Amazingly, you will see that we have removed your card: the card which you selected is not there. At this point, you might ask how we did it, or you might think, "are these guys amazing or what?" As it turns out, we are not all that amazing, just tricky. Take a careful look at Figure 4.2 and Figure 4.3. In fact, all cards shown in Figure 4.3 are different from the cards in Figure 4.2. However, when you selected your card, your brain only memorized the verbal label of the card, such as Jack of Hearts. You did not try to remember the other cards. The result is an illusion.

Figure 4.3   Your card is not there
Source: iStockPhoto.

When people don't try to specifically memorize things, they end up with quite distorted memories of the events. Two psychologists secretly recorded discussions which took place after meetings of the Cambridge Psychological Society (Hunter 1964). Two weeks later they asked participants to recall the discussions. The participants forgot more than 90% of the specific points of the discussions and the remaining 10% were substantially incorrect. Moreover, they recalled comments and details that did not happen. How would you do? Can you accurately recall the discussions you had during your team meeting last week? This example emphasizes how important it is to keep accurate records.

Although keeping accurate records is recommended by various project management procedures, it is often ignored. Even if your project team managed to create records of its meetings and other documents, would you know where these records are and have easy access to them? Though there are many good collaboration tools available that perform this function, often our memory is the only practical tool we can use. So let us learn how we can improve our ability to memorize things.

How to Improve Your Ability to Memorize

Information related to project management is often hard to memorize. If you have studied for the PMP exam, you probably agree that the PMBOK® Guide (Project Management Institute 2013) contains many general statements and descriptions of processes that are hard to remember.

How can we improve our ability to memorize information? First of all, everything depends on how you want to use this information. If you need the information for only a short period of time, you engage your short-term memory. For example, you need to enter three numbers from a spreadsheet to a project schedule:

6.435, 4.346, 5.012

Try to memorize these numbers and then, without looking at them, write them on a separate piece of paper. The easiest way to do this is to remember a verbal label associated with the numbers. Read these numbers a couple of times: six point four three five, four point three four six, and five point zero one two. You will remember these numbers only for a minute, but it will be enough to record them on a piece of paper.

However, in most cases you will need to remember information for a longer period of time. In this case, you need to associate the information with something else that you are familiar with or form associations between the different pieces of information themselves. It will help to visualize images for the various pieces of information, which may or may not have explicit relationships with this information. When you do it use the following tips (MindTools 2010; Buzan and Buzan 2010):

- Use positive, pleasant images. Your brain often blocks out unpleasant ones.

- The images may contain not only static pictures, but also movements, sounds, even smells or tastes. Engage as many senses as possible to create the most vivid impression.

- Use color or make images three dimensional; for example, if you try to memorize a block diagram or graph, use different colors for different components.

- Connect different pieces of information using a mental movie; it will help you to remember actions.

- Use symbols (traffic lights, road signs, etc.).

Here are a few memorization methods based on these ideas:

1.   **Link method**. This method can be used to memorize lists. Perhaps you need to remember phases of projects as it is described in the

PMBOK® Guide: project initiation, execution, monitoring and control, and closing out. One suggestion is to create a mental image of a person walking inside a building: opening door (initiation), walking (execution), looking at other people (monitoring and control), and leaving the building and closing the door (closing out).

2.   **Story method**. This is similar to the link method. Create a story about something you are trying to remember. Try to visualize a character or set for this story – this will make the story more vivid.

3.   **Numbering**. If you need to remember an ordered list, try to number elements of the list, even if the original list is not always numbered. For example, if you want to remember the American presidents, you may try to assign numbers to each of them. Grover Cleveland was 24th President and William McKinley was 25th.

4.   **Location method**. If information can be somehow associated with different locations, try to mentally visualize a map.

5.   **Faces method**. Try to assign an image of a person to create a relationship with the information you are trying to memorize. The person may have any relationship with the concept, even a very weak one.

6.   **Timeframe method**. If information is time related, put it visually on a timescale. Timescales do not always have to be linear. Years can be visualized as a circle, as shown on Figure 4.4. In this way, it is easier to remember durations. You can also compare events in the current and previous year, a common practice in project management. Did you know that because of the spatial positions of the hands, people often prefer conventional watches to digital watches because it makes it easier for them to assess duration?

7.   **Hierarchies and mind maps**. Try to organize information in hierarchies or mind maps, where you can create relationships between different pieces of information (Wycoff 1991; Nast 2006).

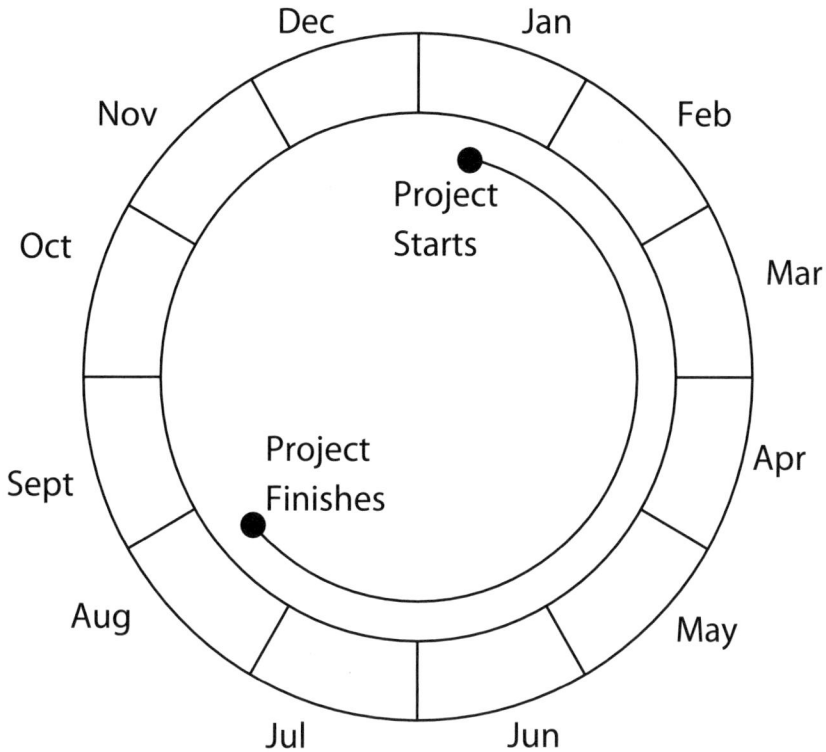

Figure 4.4   Visualization of duration

8.   **Loci method** (Higbee 2001; Yates 2001). Very often you need to memorize different words which cannot be easily associated with mental images. Imagine something familiar, such as your street or your house. Take a moment to conduct a mental walk through the rooms in your house. Ensure that you can move easily from one room to another. Along your route create a list of "loci": well-defined parts of the room such as a door, a bed, etc. When you need to memorize a list of words or ideas, you can form visual images for each of the words and place them, in order, on the loci in your route. To recall the words or ideas, you take a mental walk through your house, asking yourself, "What is on the living room door? What's in the bedroom?" And so on.

A good memory is a powerful tool for project managers; they often need to memorize different numbers, such as costs, productivity, and to recall them accurately and concisely if called upon. In most cases, this information is associated with something that can be visualized. For example, when you think about the duration of software development tasks, you may mentally associate tasks with team members.

Do Memory Exercises Actually Work?

If we spend time solving complex logical problems, such as playing Sudoku or chess, does it help to improve memory and reverse the negative effect of aging on mental abilities? The answer is apparently yes, but only to a certain extent (Aamond and Wang 2007). Apparently, mice and monkeys of all ages that are given playmates or toys will learn to complete a variety of tasks more easily than those that do not. However, these experiments were conducted with captive animals and it would be difficult to extrapolate these results to all animals and humans.

Other experiments show that elderly people who regularly perform mental exercises often improve their cognitive abilities. However, these improvements are often limited to the specific tasks they performed during their training. For example, playing Sudoku may not improve your overall mental abilities, but it will make you a better Sudoku player.

On the other hand, physical exercise has been proven to be an effective way to maintain and improve brain health. Exercise improves what scientists call "executive function," the set of abilities that allows you to select behavior that's appropriate to a situation. One of the examples of the "executive function" is the ability to focus on the job at hand in spite of distractions. Executive function usually degrades in our seventies, but physical exercise, such as fast walking, helps to maintain it. Physical exercise also helps to reduce the risk of dementia. Scientists have discovered particular neurological mechanisms which explain the effect of physical exercise on cognitive functions. So if you are a project manager, buy fitness membership for your team and yourself. It may work better than many other attempts to improve the mental abilities of your team.

Using Choice Engineering to Mitigate Memory Errors

Strange things happened with our memories. They seem to be distorted at any step: when memories are created, inside our brain, and when we recall this experience (Figure 4.5). In project management we definitely don't want to base our judgment on significantly distorted memories.

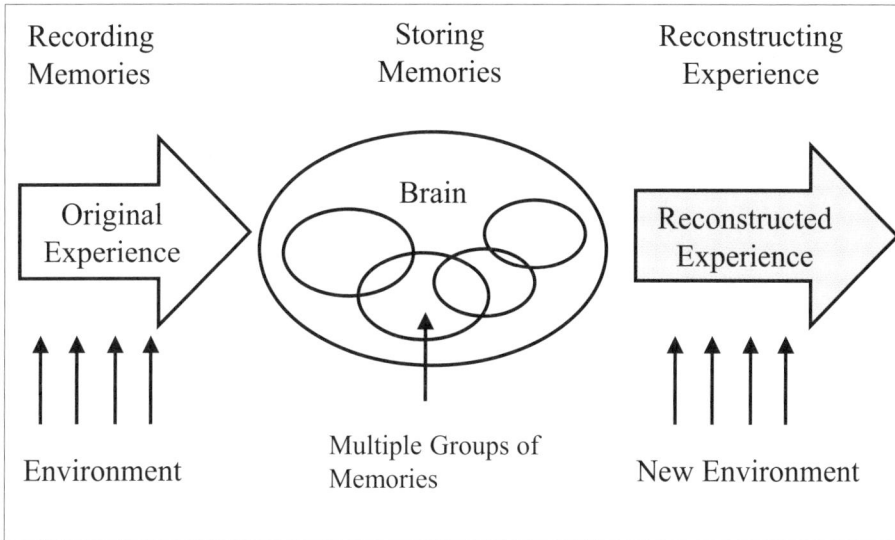

Figure 4.5   Storing and reconstructing memories

We cannot mandate project managers to improve their memory. However, we can use choice engineering as we described in Chapter 3 of this book. While we cannot completely eliminate memory errors, we can at least create an environment in which their negative impact will be mitigated. Here are a few suggestions:

1.   **Rotation**. The first suggestion is very trivial although many organizations don't follow it. Since our brain would distort our memories anyway, we need to create many experiences from different sources in such a way that they will be stored in different groups in our brain. Applying this to project management would mean that the organization should encourage people to get experience from as many different projects as possible. Not only should the project types be different, but team members should try different roles, such as engineer or project manager. Many organizations don't encourage the rotation of project managers or engineers, so they are never exposed to different projects. Very often project managers are invited from outside of an organization

or from different divisions without any experience on a particular project. Sometimes it can work. But it can cause problems, especially if a project is already under way.

2. **Industry events**. Many projects can run for years. It is hard to get different experiences if you work on one project for a long period of time. It limits memories and many memories will be combined in a limited number of groups. The solution is to go to different events, such as conferences or symposiums, or attend some training. Most companies recognize the importance of such events, but put on many conditions for employees to attend them. Some companies have a cap on the number of conferences or expenditure for training or consider these events as some sort of perk. If a company's earnings are down, they may impose various travel bans. Sometimes it happens so often that most people don't actually know when bans are lifted. Most conferences are held in nice places and include some entertainment. It is another reason why some executives think that industry events are perks. But we remember things better if they are created in a distinct and positive environment. Industry events are not perks; they are necessary to ensure high-quality projects and good company performance.

3. **Corporate knowledge base**. A number of computer tools are available to help establish a company's knowledge base. Not all companies have corporate portfolio management software, and not all companies would store project documents related to decision analysis, even if they did have the software. But there is a simple and effective way to establish a corporate knowledge base: save all your documents on a corporate intranet in such a way that they can be searched using search tools similar to Google or Bing (Virine and Trumper 2007). Just make sure you use proper keywords for your documents so that the search tool can return the most relevant documents.

SMART TIPS
- Using mental images associated with information we are trying to remember is an efficient way to memorize information.
- Memory is not a time capsule in the brain, preserved intact for posterity. Your memories can be distorted or augmented by context: the way the questions are framed, by current experience, etc. Memories are reconstructed when we withdraw information. To reduce potential memory errors, organizations should expose employees to different types of projects and different roles.
- Attending industry events and training is proven to be an efficient way to reduce memory errors.
- Create a corporate knowledge base using simple off-the-shelf computer tools.

5

Emotions in Project Management

In this chapter we will learn about how decisions in project management are affected by our emotions. People make choices under the influence of emotions all the time. Emotions can lead to mental mistakes; mental mistakes, as we have already learned, lead to low-quality decisions. In this chapter, we will not attempt a comprehensive review of human emotions; instead, we will explain why even the most emotionally intelligent people make irrational decisions when they find themselves in stressful situations. We will also provide a few choice engineering ideas that will help you to mitigate the negative impact of emotions on your decisions in project management.

The Head-butt Felt Around the World

What was your most memorable moment of the 2006 football World Cup in Germany? If you are like us, it was the moment during the final match between France and Italy where France's captain, national hero, and talisman Zinedine Zidane, playing in his final match for France, was sent off in disgrace for giving Italy's Marco Materazzi a head-butt in retaliation for a series of verbal insults the Italian had barraged him with. Italy won 5–3 on penalties. Millions of his fans all around the world were left wondering how such an experienced player as Zinedine Zidane was goaded into acting so recklessly. Though there was some insinuation that Materazzi had managed to go as low as mentioning Zidane's mother, it did not justify Zidane's actions.

We can imagine what happened to Zidane at this moment. It was extra time in perhaps the most important game of his career. France was on the verge of repeating as World Cup champions, an achievement that would place them in very rare company in the annals of soccer greats. It is in this type of environment, where the pressure to succeed is so great, that even seasoned performers find it very difficult to perform at their best. Strangely, the object that most affects their performance is not a tall, foul-mouthed Italian soccer star, or some other external force; it is a small organ located deep in our brains, the amygdala (Swanson and Petrovich 1998, Whalen and Phelps 2009). The amygdala is an almond-shaped group of nuclei located deep within the medial temporal lobes of the brain. The primary purpose of the amygdala is the processing and memory of emotional reactions. When people perceive danger or become involved in other situations which cause fear or anger, a signal is sent to the amygdala, where an association with a memory of the stimuli is formed. The signal is then passed to other portions of the brain, which triggers a response to the danger. This response can cause different symptoms: rapid heartbeat, increased respiration, stress-hormone release, and even temporary freezing. In addition, people's ability to process information rationally becomes very limited for a period of time. This period of irrationality can be just few seconds, a few minutes, or longer depending on the individual and situation. During this period of time, people will make decisions based on emotion rather than analysis. Essentially, during times of high stress, our amygdala sets off our instinctive defense mechanisms significantly faster than they can be shut down.

This mechanism was developed in the brains of our remote ancestors millions and millions of years ago and helped protect our predecessors from the many dangers they faced in the hostile environments in which they lived. Nowadays, the perceived threats in the environment are different; instead of a terrifying encounter with a large carnivore during the early Pleistocene, it may be a terrifying encounter with a senior project manager. Regardless of the perceived threat, our reaction to danger remains the same. Perhaps the same process took over Zidane just before the infamous incident, when under increasing stress a cascade of signals from his amygdala overwhelmed Zidane's ability to think rationally and led to the delivery of the head-butt and his eventual ignominious dismissal from the match (Figure 5.1).

It is important to note that everyone, from presidents to janitors, is susceptible to the same symptoms. If you happen to come across someone who is completely unaffected by emotions, there are two possible explanations: you are on the set of a *Star Trek* movie and are looking at an actor playing a Vulcan, or you have stumbled upon a corpse. This is not to deny that there are differences in individuals' ability to handle stress and act appropriately in stressful situations. However, even for those people who are able to maintain the best control, they too will eventually succumb to their own biology and start to make instinctive or irrational choices. Often this is triggered not by simple stimuli, as in a clearly defined threat, but in complex situations where the real threat is to themselves or, in the case of project managers, to their projects.

Figure 5.1   Why did Zinedine Zidane head-butt Marco Materazzi?
Source: Alex Alexeev.

Our Emotional Choices Often are Not the Best Ones

Pavel I was a Russian emperor from 1796 to 1801 and often made emotional choices. His foul moods and emotional nature is the stuff of legend. One day, as was the case on most days, he woke up in a bad mood. As he stood in his bedroom, he looked out of the window with a view of the palace ground. As he surveyed his ground, he happened to spot a particularly unfortunate fellow, "Look at that person. He dares to walk near the palace without showing any sign of respect, he should at least take off his hat," he pointed out to a few of his courtiers who were standing attentively about his royal person, looking for any chance to curry favor as was their custom. Upon hearing this, his attendants with intimate knowledge of Pavel's emotional character, instantly issued the emperor's decree that any and all subjects who passed by a palace must take off their hat in a show of respect to their sovereign. As often happens in project management, publishing edicts or regulations and actually getting everyone to follow them are two completely different things. To ensure everyone followed the new decree, the emperor's courtiers tasked the police with enforcing it, which they did with stern language and judicious use of fists, boots, and whatever else brought about the desired behavior.

After a few months, the new project was deemed a complete success. Doffing their hats as a show of respect became a habit for the locals. As things would have it, Pavel was again looking out of his windows, this time in a better mood. He happened to see one of his subjects removing his hat as he walked by the palace; puzzled since this seemed to be unusual behavior, he turned to his courtiers, "How strange," he observed, "I just saw someone take off their hat as they walked by, has spring arrived early?" "But it is according to your wishes, sire," they replied. "I did not say such a thing," said Pavel. Typically, like many of us, Pavel does not have a good memory of decisions made when we are emotional; often we cannot remember them at all. With this new understanding of their ruler's wishes, his underlings quickly set out to repeal the previous decree, but, predictably, undoing the decree proved as difficult as imposing it in the first place and the policemen were again sent out to enforce the new/old regulation: everyone must now keep their hat on as they passed by the palace.

Many project managers follow in Pavel's footsteps and make emotional decisions. If something is wrong with a project, instead of taking the time to carefully analyze the underlying cause, they prefer to act quickly. Often applying the scattershot technique when applying blame, if you throw enough around, some of it will stick. Bugs in the software? It is QA's fault. If they didn't persist in testing so much, there would not be as many bugs in the code. If we reduce QA resources, we will have fewer issues to fix and we can meet our product launch date. Then they ask themselves why they did not come up with this simple, cost-saving solution before.

Here is a true story. A Canadian high-tech company designed small TV sets to be installed in front of each exercise machine in fitness clubs. Each set had a screen and keypad to change channels, volume and so on. Originally, all the keypads were supposed to use bubbly buttons, sticking out from the keypad. One day the company CEO, a businessman, not a project manager or hardware engineer, demonstrated the device to somebody very influential in the fitness industry. This person had read somewhere about an experiment that demonstrated that bubbly buttons were less durable than flat buttons. Apparently, somebody had pressed on a bubbly button 1 million times and it stopped working and, in addition, made the claim that flat buttons were more durable. On that same day, the CEO went back to his office and requested a redesign of the keypad with flat buttons. Interestingly, nobody, including the CEO and engineers, knew anything about the actual experiment with the 1 million button clicks. But it was the CEO's order and the engineers started the new development. Later on, when the whole project was delayed, the CEO discovered that the reason was his own request to redesign a keypad. Similarly to Emperor Pavel I, the CEO was quite surprised. He asked why the engineers did not provide him with cost and duration estimates. As it happens, the CEO was told that the redesign and changing of suppliers would mean changes to the project cost and schedule. But he was so emotional on that day that he was unable to use or recall any of the advice or estimates any of his project team had provided.

If you find that people around you are making decisions that seem stupid, irrational, counterproductive (you name it), there is a good chance that it is because of their emotions. Getting angry with them will not help and may exacerbate the issue. Remember that, given time, their emotions will return to a normal state and at that time they may see in retrospect that their actions were rash and they have the option to change their decisions.

Emotional Intelligence

> *Emotional intelligence is the ability and capacity to manage and control your own emotions as well as the emotions of others.*

So how can we minimize the effect of emotions on our project management decisions? In other words, how can we be emotionally intelligent so that we can manage our own and our team's emotions? There are a number of different models of emotional intelligence. One of them was offered by Daniel Goleman

(2006) and adopted for project management by Anthony Mercino (2007). This emotional intelligence model has five domains:

1.   self-awareness

2.   self-management

3.   social awareness

4.   relationship management

5.   team leadership.

First of all, we need to identify these emotions, as shown in Figure 5.2 (Baucells and Sarin 2008a). It is important to note that mental mistakes and consequent wrong decisions are caused not only by negative emotions, but also positive ones, such as passion or love. As we all know, people in love can be very delusional and are prone to irrational choices.

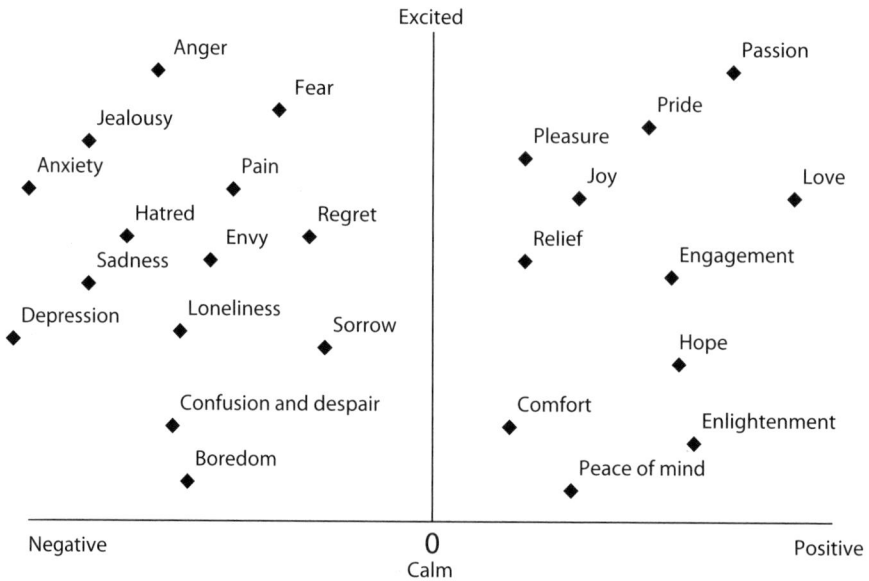

Figure 5.2   Emotions

You also need to recognize the impact of emotions on our intuitive or "gut feeling" decisions. This is called self-awareness. You are probably aware that if you are angry, you may say something that you wish you hadn't. Therefore, you need to be able to control your emotions; this is called self-management. As a part of a social network, which in the case of a project is the project team, you must be able to recognize other people's emotions. Finally, and perhaps the most difficult skill to master, you must learn how to manage other people's emotions through relationship management and team leadership.

Some people may be extremely intelligent, but at the same time have a low emotional intelligence. This explains why so many fraud artists are successful at separating normally intelligent people from their money. Various Ponzi schemes, real estate fraud, and other such criminal activities are successful because of the manner in which they manipulate our emotions. In 2005, the Ig Nobel Award in Literature was given to the Internet entrepreneurs of Nigeria, for distributing by email a bold series of short stories, thus introducing millions of readers to a cast of rich characters – Barrister Jon A. Mbeki Esq., General Sani Abacha, Mrs. Mariam Sanni Abacha, and others – each of whom requires just a small amount of expense money so as to obtain access to the great wealth to which they are entitled and which they would like to share with the kind person who assists them (Ig Nobel 2010). In fact, the emails were written well enough that they were able to trigger one of the most powerful emotions: greed. Greed is a good example of an emotion that can cause a mental mistake: "If I send a little bit of money to Mrs. Mariam Sanni Abacha, I will be rich." The thought of easy money may generate a very powerful image of a Palm Beach villa, or some other wealthy enclave in your mind. How do we know this? Obviously the emails were successful, otherwise these unappreciated literature gems would have long ago disappeared from our inboxes.

You may think that Mrs. Mariam Sanni Abacha-type events may not be applicable to project management: the case is too obvious and intelligent project managers would recognize it. But even in large projects, where detailed analysis should serve as a counterweight to our propensity for rash decision, project managers sometimes demonstrate very little emotional intelligence. In 2000, Apache, Beau Canada, and Murphy Oil announced a major discovery in the Ladyfern gas field located in the very remote north-eastern region of British Columbia, Canada. Major discoveries are rare in the mature Western Canada region. Ladyfern drew international attention because of huge production rates of test wells. The initial high production made the gas field's economic potential seem extremely lucrative, causing many gas producers to jump on the bandwagon. Land lease prices increased dramatically, construction of an expensive pipeline started. This area can be developed only during winter months when the roads are accessible. Therefore, in order to be first on the ground, some companies spent millions to deliver crews and equipment by helicopter. It was a real gold rush. Production from this field grew in 2001, but then fell sharply: Ladyfern was not as large as originally estimated and gas producers operating in this area incurred major losses (Andrews 2009). While engineers and managers of oil companies are very intelligent people, it is the lack of emotional intelligence that leads them to Ladyfern-type losses.

How to Become Emotionally Intelligent: A Choice Engineering Approach

There are many self-help books that that offer advice on how to manage your emotions: there are many professionals who specialize in helping people with emotional problems. Obviously we cannot and do not want to compete with them; rather, our goal is to give you some basic ideas on how to avoid being subject to emotional errors that can affect your projects.

Since we cannot mandate anybody to become emotionally intelligent, these are some non-intrusive ways to avoid decision-making while under the sway of emotions. They belong to the choice engineering principles which we discussed in Chapter 3.

COOLING PERIOD

On October 19, 1987, a date also known as Black Monday, stock markets all over the world collapsed (Browning 2007). In particular, the Dow Jones Industrial Average plummeted 508 points, losing 22.6% of its value in one day. Interestingly, no definitive conclusions have been reached on the reasons behind the 1987 crash. One of the consequences of the 1987 crash was the introduction of a cooling period on the NYSE. This mandatory market shutdown is triggered whenever a large predefined market decline occurs during the trading day. This shutdown is meant to inhibit the effect of investors' emotions. Typically, investors are driven by two strong emotions: greed and fear. Remember how the amygdala shuts down rational thought and people make decisions based on the mental mistakes that their emotions generate. The concept is to not allow people to make investment decisions for a period of time after a crisis situation. The same suggestion is very useful when we talk about self-management.

If you are in a stressful situation, give yourself a timeout until your level of stress-related hormones declines before you make any decisions. The old advice to count to 10 before you say anything turns out to be quite sound. But, it is easier said than done; deciding not to decide is also a decision, which you will have to do under stress.

IN A CRISIS, USE PREDEFINED ROUTINES

You have probably participated in a fire drill in your office. If you take a cruise, you will probably be asked to participate in a drill where you are familiarized with the life-saving procedures on the ship. All these drills are very simple: just walk to a certain area when an alarm sounds. So why bother to practice? Unfortunately, during a real crisis, such as a fire, our ability to make rational choices will be impaired by emotions. If we can practice our routines that we will use during crisis, it should become automatic. When they become automatic, our decisions will be made based on memory, which will have the mental images of the drills we practiced.

We are constantly involved in activities which can cause strong emotional responses. It is better to prepare for these types of activity in advance. For example, airport security procedures are not very pleasant: take off your coat, take off your shoes, remove your laptop, remove any metal from your pockets, place everything in the bins, keep the boarding pass in your hands, and walk through the metal detector. Moreover, this procedure has gradually become more and more complex. If you are not a frequent flyer and used to these inconveniences, you may find yourself stressed out. What could happen? You may forget your watch or phone at the security check. Worse, you may appear suspicious and attract unwanted attention, and we all know where that leads. However, if you plan in advance by simply thinking about how many things you need to take out and place back, the chance that you may lose something will be reduced.

In project management this process is called risk response planning (Project Management Institute 2013, Heldman 2005, Kendrick 2009). Instead of panicking about defects that have been discovered close to a software release date and deciding to get rid of your QA team, it would be better to plan some time in advance to fix any bugs that are found late in the development cycle. Moreover, it is important that realistic buffers or contingencies for bug fixing are included in the baseline schedule as part of standard practices for all software development projects in organizations.

TALK IT OUT

Psychologists have found that one of the best responses to an emotional situation is to talk with someone. You do not even need to have a clear goal in mind; just the act of talking with another person reduces the level of stress-related hormones and helps you to start thinking rationally again. Psychologists recommend different types of support groups in cases of crisis: when people talk with each other, it helps them to cope with their problems.

Unfortunately we often forget about this simple way to manage emotional situations in project management. Sales are significantly down and senior management is very upset. What do project managers often do? They sit in their office firing off emails, perhaps some of them containing irrational orders. What is a better solution? Simple: call a team meeting. First, the meeting itself will act as cooling-down period that is necessary to reduce levels of emotion. During this meeting, every member of the team, even those who are not directly involved in the sales process, should have their turn to express an opinion. The goal is not to make a decision at this time, but to allow emotions to cool off and help make rational decisions later.

SMART TIPS

Humans have developed complex neurological mechanisms to react on external stimuli through emotions. The emotional response often leads to illusions and wrong decisions. Here are a few simple ideas to manage emotional response in project management:

- Set up cooling-off periods in case of crisis before any significant decisions should be made.
- Plan responses to potential crisis situations in advance.
- Start meaningful and extensive discussions within a team if a crisis situation has occurred.

6

Behavioral Traps

> *The most important thing in project management is not to become entrapped.*
>
> *Mickey Mouse*

You are driving down a highway, and as usual, you have chosen the fast lane. However, today, it seems to be moving more slowly than usual and when you glance to the side, the adjacent lane appears to be moving faster. After five minutes without improvement, you are starting to wonder whether you should switch lanes, but because you have already spent some time in what is normally the fast lane, you hope that it will eventually resume its normal pace. Essentially, you have become entrapped. In this chapter we will discuss behavioral traps or situations where people become engaged in a rational course of actions which later become undesirable.

Sunk Cost

Here is an example of how you could become entrapped during the execution of a project: You are the promoter for a new Hollywood horror movie *79 Vampires and Anxious Housewives*. You have already invested $20 million in marketing and, despite an ocean of blood, the movie sucked at the box office. Apparently the vampires were less scary than your average HR director and the werewolves sounded more like a high school hip hop band. Your best bet to recoup your losses is DVD sales. You have the following choices:

a) Spend an additional $10 million on an aggressive marketing campaign: "Buy *79 Vampires* on DVD or you will be their victim." Leave out the part that the real victimization occurs when they pay over their hard-earned dollars for this dud.

b) Spend $1 million on a poster campaign: "Always have 79 vampires at your home."

    c)   Walk away. Don't invest another dime in this money pit. Instead, invest it in a new romantic comedy *Frankenstein Resurrection IV*.

What would you choose? You have already spent $20 million – wouldn't it be nice to see some return on that investment? It would be very difficult just to walk away, refuse to spend another dime on it. Unfortunately, spending more money on an already bad investment will probably just increase your losses. This is called the *sunk cost* effect. Sunk costs are a trap because it is difficult to ignore the temptation to spend more money on a losing project to try to improve the outcome. Because of the sunk cost effect, people often elect to spend more money when the better response would be to walk away.

> *Sunk cost is past costs or efforts that have already been incurred and cannot be recovered.*

The sunk cost trap affects every type of decision, both large and small. The Constellation Program is a human spaceflight program that was designed to replace the Space Shuttle and send astronauts to the Moon and possibly to Mars as well. The Constellation Program included the Ares I and Ares V booster rockets (Figure 6.1), the Orion crew capsule, the Altair lunar lander, and other components.

In 2010 President Barack Obama found that the project was too costly, "behind schedule, and lacking in innovation" (Amos 2010). Former astronauts Neil Armstrong, James Lovell and Eugene Cernan urged President Obama not to cancel and warned that it would be a "devastating" new policy for the future of NASA (MSNBC News 2010). In particular, they mentioned the $10 billion-plus in investments that would be lost if the program was canceled. In fact, $10 billion had already been spent. To continue to invest funds in a program that was not providing the results that were promised would be wasteful. Actually, the faster that ineffective programs or projects are canceled the better off we will all be. In the case of the Constellation Program, the solution was to either cancel the program or to significantly change its scope. Barack Obama later announced major changes to the program that would focus on human flight to Mars, while the Orion capsule would be used as a rescue spacecraft for the International Space Station.

Figure 6.1　Launch of Aries prototype October 28, 2009

Source: NASA/Sandra Joseph and Kevin O'Connell.

One of the main issues in project management is related to managers who often do not realize the magnitude of an issue. They believe that the issue can be addressed within the framework of the existing design or solution; therefore, they perform incremental and often futile attempts to fix the project rather than start all over again. This type of situation occurred during the construction of Russia's longest railroad tunnel, the Severomuysky Tunnel (15,343 meters, or 50,338 feet) in Siberia. Construction started in 1978 (Levinsky 2003) and soon after it was discovered that the mountain through which the tunnel would pass had a large number of faults with pressurized water, sand, and clay. Tunneling in such faults cannot be done by traditional methods and attempts to tunnel though one of the faults caused a collapse of the face of the tunnel, several deaths, and a major delay in construction. In addition to these troubles, the tunnel was located in a seismically active region. Some experts suggested that perhaps it would have been better to stop construction and build the tunnel in a more suitable environment. However, after each setback, it appears that key decision-makers had a thought process that went something like this:

> Yes. We had a problem. But next time it will work because our technology is improving and we have more experience with these problems.

Unfortunately it was wishful thinking. Although tunneling methods and technology gradually improved, it did not compensate for the huge delays and cost overruns caused by the initial conditions. The longer the project continued, the more difficult it became to escape from the sunk cost trap. The tunnel was finally completed 25 years late: 31 people lost their lives during construction.

To overcome behavioral traps, awareness is the best defense. Here are some specific suggestions about how we can manage the sunk cost effect (Hammond et al. 2002):

1.   Ask advice from project managers or engineers who were not involved in past decisions because these people will be less likely to be committed to these decisions.

2.   Try to understand why you are motivated to continue to follow earlier poor decisions; remember, being smart or experienced does not make you immune to mental errors.

3.   Project managers or engineers who were part of the previous
       decisions should either recuse themselves or have less involvement
       in the subsequent decisions. For example, if a bank gives a loan and
       the borrower has difficulties in paying it back, the bank often gives
       additional funds to help the borrower recover. While this sometimes
       works, it often leads to more bad loans, which in turn are harder to
       recover. Researchers found that if the bank manager who issues the
       original loan and the manager who approves additional funding
       are different people, the chance of a default on this loan is lower.

Time Bombs

A common strategy of businesses is to lure us to buy their products by offering
"buy now – pay later" options, a strategy that is very popular with consumers.
In the early 2000s, the U.S. government modified mortgage regulations that
lowered requirements for mortgage approvals in an effort to boost home
ownership. For many people this experiment has become a trap: they took out
mortgages that are beyond their means to pay off. The cumulative effect of this
time trap was one of the prime causes of the worst financial crisis since the
1930s. People rarely think about the long-term consequences of their decisions
and become entrapped: drug users think about short-term pleasure, but not
long-term addiction; people who enjoy their favorite dessert every day do not
consider the possibility of becoming obese; and, software developers who fail
to spend the time to document their source code do not realize that they will
not understand their own software the next year. This effect is often referred to
as a *time delay trap*.

Here is another example of a time bomb. At the beginning of a project
decisions are made about the proper course of action that will define the project.
However, if the timeframe of the project is long, the situation may change and
a previously decided course of action may no longer be optimal or valid. The
Mackenzie Valley Pipeline was supposed to transport natural gas from the
Beaufort Sea and Mackenzie Delta through Canada's Northwest Territories to
Alberta. The Mackenzie River delta contains huge deposits of oil and gas, so in
2004 several large oil companies and aboriginal groups put forward a proposal
to build a multi-billion-dollar pipeline (CBC News 2009). The problem is that
for a project of this magnitude the assessment, design, and approval process
takes such a long time that conditions can change dramatically. The balance
between supply and demand may shift multiple times one way or another.

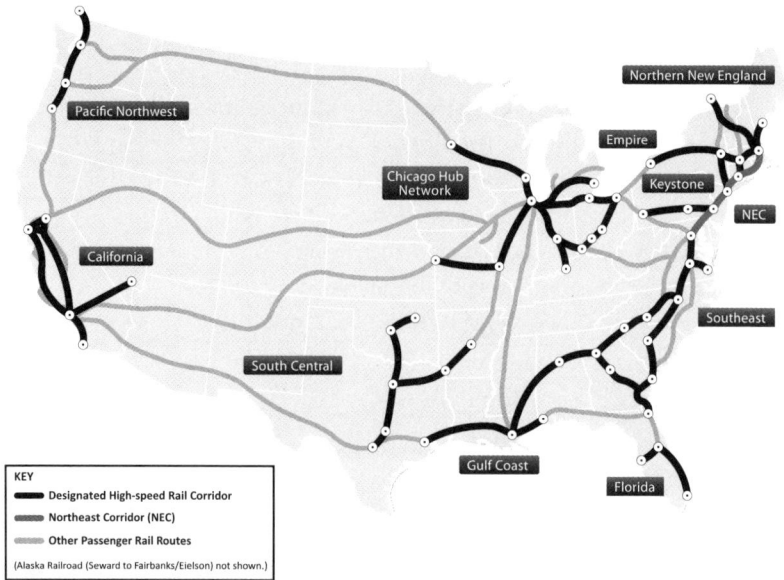

Figure 6.2   Vision for high-speed rail in America
Source: Federal Railroad Administration.

One major shift has been the emergence of shale gas in North America. New techniques have made the extraction of what was previously a very expensive and marginal resource very competitive in comparison with traditional natural gas resources. In addition, in many regions, shale gas is located very close to the areas of the consumption, such as Appalachia, and does not require the construction of new major pipelines. Because of this and other developments in the economy, the Mackenzie Valley Pipeline project could change radically or not be required at all. This is called the *deterioration trap*.

What can we do about time delay and deterioration traps? Here are a few suggestions based on the choice engineering approach:

1.   Always ask yourself the question: if I do something now, what could change over time and how will these changes affect my original decision?

2.   Whenever possible, try not to make decisions that will not have consequences for a long period of time. For example, instead of investing hundreds of billions immediately on the design and construction of high-speed trains and infrastructure, the US

government has chosen a gradual approach (Glasser 2009). They invest in projects that will have an immediate impact on the rail system, such as system upgrades that will help existing trains travel faster. At the same time, these projects should create a foundation for future high-speed trains (Figure 6.2).

3.   Do not make irreversible decisions. If the situation changes, you must be able to make corrections or even abandon a project at minimum cost. For example, if you develop a software package, do not attempt to implement all possible features before taking it to the market. Develop in phases and ensure that you set in place the foundation that will allow you to provide incremental improvements in the future as required. In fact, one of the fundamental principles of agile project management is iterative development.

Prudence Traps

A number of years ago U.S. automakers were updating their sales projections (Hammond et al. 2002). They asked different departments within their companies to forecast sales, inventories, costs, and other variables. Each department came up with a very conservative forecast (from their point of view at least): produce enough cars to ensure that they can meet demand. However, corporate planners used this data at face value and then made their own adjustment, just to be on the safe side, to ensure that they could meet demand. As a result, automakers produced so many cars that most sat in the car lots for up to six months and required substantial cuts in prices before they were actually sold. This is called the *prudence trap*. Some project managers still plan and manage their projects based on "worst-case scenarios." While it can be important to have conservative estimates, sometimes it is more important to be honest and make a realistic assessment of the probabilities of future events. The prudence trap can lead to cascading effects with disastrous consequences.

Collective Traps

Approximately 40% of the world's oil production is controlled by 12 countries that belong to the Organization of the Petroleum Exporting Countries (OPEC). When prices are low, OPEC issues quotas for their members and they reduce supply until the prices rebound. While this could work in theory, in reality since OPEC does not control 60% of oil production, its power to control prices is limited. When OPEC reduces production and prices go up, this provides an opportunity for other producers, such as Mexico, Russia, or Norway, to increase production and capitalize on higher prices at the expense of OPEC members. The problem oil producers face is if each country acts according to its own self-interest, everybody will suffer. This effect is sometimes called a *collective trap*, because it involves a number of people with different agendas who interact but do not necessarily fully communicate with each other (Plous 1993). A typical example of a collective trap is rush-hour traffic. Everybody hits the road around 5 p.m. because it is convenient. But as a result of the heavy traffic, everybody suffers. Mathematicians research such traps using *game theory*, which is a mathematical theory of human behavior in competitive situations in which players interact.

Game theory seeks to understand and explain a number of similar problems. Let us assume that you have a job interview. Everything was going well and it looked like you would land the job. But the final question posed a dilemma for you: "What is your salary expectation?" You do not know how much the company is willing to pay for this position. If you ask too much, you might not get an offer. If you ask too little, you may lose a significant amount of money for years to come. You become entrapped. Ideally, you could dodge the question, but you probably will have to come up with a figure.

Collective traps occur in project management all the time. The relationships between customers and developers often lead to a collective trap when both sides do not clearly state their expectations. Organizations could be entrapped in complex relationships between management and employees as well as different departments and business units.

How can we avoid collective traps and similar traps regarding interactions between different groups of people? Since it is impossible to eliminate traps and prohibit people from falling into traps, choice engineering principles can be applied. In the late 1950s, the U.S. and Soviet Union had no effective communications with each other. Instead, they were forced to assume the intentions of each other, a process which eventually brought both countries to the brink of nuclear war. Fortunately one of the leading researchers in game theory, Thomas Schelling, had close contact with the Kennedy and, later, Johnson administrations and introduced Robert Kennedy to his war games (Harford 2008). Based on this analysis, Thomas Schelling realized that a full-blown nuclear war could be triggered as the result of a mistake by a radar operator or simple misunderstanding. In 1958, he proposed to establish a communication hotline between the United States and Soviet Union which contributed to reducing the threat of nuclear war. Thomas Schelling got a Nobel Prize in economics in 2005.

Effective communication, while sounding trivial, is not easy to establish. It is a key aspect of all project management education and is mentioned in the PMBOK® Guide (Project Management Institute 2013) numerous times. One of the fundamental concepts of agile project management is face-to-face communication (Manifesto 2006). At the same time, a lot of problems occur because communication channels are ineffective, slow, one-way (down), or even completely shut down.

Homeland Security's virtual fence project was an example of how ineffective communication between contractors and users would lead to project delays and cost overruns (Widman 2008). Users, members of the U.S. Border Patrol, were excluded from the project process. The project started in 2006, but a year later Congress learned that it was delayed because project complexity was underestimated. In particular, radar equipment that was supposed to detect illegal aliens crossing the border did not work in bad weather; cameras used to snap pictures of the aliens sent back very low-quality images if the distance to the subject was greater than 3.1 miles; the virtual fence communication system interfered with local residents' wireless networks.

SMART TIPS

Behavioral traps are situations when people decide upon a rational course of action which later becomes undesirable. To protect against sunk cost, time bombs, collective and other traps:

- Admit mistakes and encourage the same as part of your organization's culture.
- Minimize damage to project outcomes by reversing incorrect decisions as quickly as possible.
- Use effective communication as a defense again collective traps.

7

Heuristics and Biases

As we go about our lives, whenever we make decisions, whether they are relatively important – "what strategies or tactics should we use to reduce project cost?" – or relatively trivial – "is No-Name peanut butter really a better bargain than the brand-name version?" – we are forced to assess probabilities or essentially make bets, which is not an easy task. We often apply rules of thumb or heuristics when we make judgments about probabilities of future events. In many cases, using these rules will help us make good decisions. However, depending upon the situation, this type of decision-making can lead to faulty judgments or biases. We have already covered some of these biases previously in this book; however, in this chapter we will focus on a few common heuristics and biases which affect project management: availability, anchoring, representativeness, and others.

How Project Managers Became "Gamblers"

There is a problem that pervades our society: we have all become pathological gamblers. We are not referring to those who spend all of their spare time in casinos in the vague hope that they will win their retirement nest egg – the opposite outcome is almost always the case. Rather, we are referring to how we must gamble during the course of our everyday lives. If you drive or are a passenger in a car, there is a probability that you will be involved in an accident. Take your clothes to the dry cleaner and there is a probability that your shirt will be damaged; you buy chicken in the supermarket and there is a probability you will get salmonella or some other unpleasant condition. In fact, there are whole industries whose revenue and profits dwarfs those of the Las Vegas casinos that are all based on gambling: investments and insurance. When we invest our money, what we are actually doing is gambling that certain stocks or mutual funds will provide us with a certain return. And unless we are willing to watch the value of our savings evaporate over time due to inflation, we are left with few options but to place a bet using one or multiple financial instruments. In our society, this type of gambling is both a respectable profession and a source of great personal wealth. Professional gamblers earn a much higher amount of money than people who actually produce the goods. Twenty of the 120 richest people in the world made their fortune in investment, finance, or leveraged buyouts – industries that are based on gambling (Forbes 2012).

Perhaps what is most interesting is that this type of gambling has in some specific cases become mandatory; you must bet on something or face possible legal consequences. The most common example is car insurance, which you must have before you can drive on public roads. As this is the case and we don't have any other option but to gamble, let's learn how to improve our gambling skills. In this chapter we will learn about common mistakes which all people, including project managers, make when people make their choices under uncertainties.

Availability Heuristic

Let's imagine that you are an IT project manager and tasked with selecting new laptop computers for your organization. You reviewed all the product sheets for Dell, Toshiba, HP, and other laptop brands: performance, price, reliability, memory, etc. After a detailed analysis, you decided that Toshiba is the best brand for your organization. However, the day before you are planning to issue your recommendation, you meet a friend in a local pub. After you mention your plans to recommend Toshiba, he gave you a funny look and then said: "Don't do it, I bought a Toshiba and after only three months the hard drive failed and I lost all of my data. This is a terrible computer." You are slightly flummoxed and you start to rethink your proposed recommendation of Toshiba laptops; perhaps Dell would be the better choice. Here is the problem. You did your analysis using comprehensive information about each laptop; however, after a chance meeting at the pub, you are now thinking of ignoring the results of your analysis because now your assessment of the reliability of certain brands of computers is skewed (Schwartz 2005). In reality, your friend describes only one single case with a particular Toshiba computer and does not reflect any statistical data about the quality and reliability of said laptop.

Here are some other common examples:

- When avid smokers are asked why they do not try to get rid of their habit despite overwhelming evidence that smoking is harmful, they may answer that they aren't worried because they know someone who smoked all of their life and lived until the ripe old age of 95, when they were unfortunately run over by a bus.

- You decide to take a vacation in Mexico and, during your research to find the perfect vacation locale, you discover that Mexico has beautiful beaches, world-class hotels, and good security in the tourist areas. However, just as you were in the process of selecting your Mexican vacation destination, you see a headline in the news that a US tourist has been robbed in Acapulco. You become extremely worried and think about cancelling your vacation.

- You are planning to start developing a database application and need to select a platform. You know only four companies that develop software applications similar to the one you are planning to develop. Three of them are using Oracle and only one is using Microsoft SQL Server, so you decide on using the Oracle platform.

What is the common theme in all of these examples? In all of these situations you are making a bet. If you smoke, you are betting that you will be one of the lucky few whose life will not be shortened by the habit. If you purchase a computer, you are betting that it will be reliable. Unfortunately, most people don't perform this type of detailed analysis for most real-life issues in which the extra effort would be very beneficial. One of the main reasons we don't is because it takes a lot of mental effort and energy. In addition, our ability to perform a truly rational analysis is limited because:

a)   the information we have may be limited

b)   our minds have basic cognitive limitations, and

c)   there is only a finite amount of time that we have to make decisions.

Therefore instead of using detailed analysis, we rely on simplified mental strategies or "rules of thumb" to guide our decisions. In the psychology of judgment and decision-making, these rules of thumb are called *heuristics*. In many cases, heuristics lead to good decisions; however, they often cause inconsistencies and predictable biases.

The behaviors we describe for car-buying and smoking are examples of one such heuristic: *availability* (Tversky and Kahneman 1973). According to this heuristic, people make judgments about the probability of certain events based on how easily the event is brought to their mind. When people bet or take other risks, they have to determine the probability of some type of event occurring. And they often do it incorrectly:

- Medical statistics are a reliable way to estimate the lifespan of smokers vs. non-smokers. But a couple of examples of smokers we know who lived until the age of 95 can cause us to disregard the medical statistics. As a result we may significantly reduce the probability of experiencing a shorter lifespan because of smoking.

- When you read about one instance of a robbery in Acapulco you didn't read about the hundreds of thousands of successful vacations and happy tourists. To make matters worse, because there are no images of the actual robbery, you tend to make them up, enhance them with images you might have seen in movies: lots of violence, blood, incompetent local police in cahoots with organized crime. Now the previous images in your mind of a relaxing vacation on the beach are replaced with the images of an imagined crime scene. No wonder you are thinking of canceling your trip to Acapulco.

- You know about only four organizations that are developing software similar to the application you have planned; however, there are probably dozens if not hundreds of companies involved in similar development. You are making a decision based on a very limited number of samples.

In all of these situations, people judge the frequency of an event based on something that is easy to remember or imagine, but not actual data. Essentially we replace statistics with imagination.

Here is another example of the availability heuristic. Let's compare two different descriptions of potential oil drilling failure due to the low quality of seismic data (Table 7.1).

Table 7.1   Compare two descriptions of potential oil drilling failure

If high-quality seismic data is not purchased, there is an increased chance that the well we drill will be dry and we will incur some losses.	If high-quality seismic data is not purchased, a $3.6 million well may be dry. Moreover, we will have wasted at least 17 business days drilling plus three more days on rig mobilization. In addition, we will miss the opportunity to drill wells in a different field. We estimate that our income after taxes will be 10% lower if this well is dry.

Which version of the event will sound more realistic to the management? If you are like most managers, you picked the second. It is more vivid, has more details, and therefore looks more probable. Vivid events are easily brought to mind and since we can recall them better, it affects our estimation of probabilities. Lawyers, police officers, and politicians often use the availability heuristic and paint vivid descriptions of a process or an event when trying to convince us that their version of events is the truth. Experienced project managers are also aware that they can sway senior management or project stakeholders by painting vivid pictures – for example, a project failure if additional resources are not provided.

The availability heuristic is in great evidence in project management. For example, when we estimate project cost, duration, or resources, we are doing it based on previous instances of similar projects or tasks. Because very few organizations keep an actual lessons learned database, project managers or schedulers are often left with only their own memory to try and recall these previous projects. They imagine what could happen in their projects and, based on this, estimate the probability of future events. Sometimes they are able to perform quite accurate assessments, but if they only remember extreme events (successes or failures), or events associated with vivid details, their estimates can be skewed.

So, how can you mitigate the negative impact of availability heuristic? The choice engineering-type suggestion is to collect as many samples of reliable information and include it in the analysis. For example, if you estimate probability of a risk "delay with receiving payment," ask your accounting department to check records of previous payments – have they been delayed or not? If you don't obtain this information, you may base your judgment on a recent payment delay or a remarkable delay which involved a huge sum of money.

Anchoring

Do you know how much this seemingly simple purse cost (Figure 7.1)? The price usually starts at about US$5,000, but can reach five- and sometimes six-digit prices. It is a "Birkin" bag by Hermes. Allegedly, the waiting list for a Birkin is over two years; however, Hermes will sell a Birkin to "regular" customers without putting them through the agony of a waiting list. Hermes claims that only a few hundred bags are produced per year and that they are sold only at Hermes stores and never online. The bags are often constructed using exotic animal skins and studded with diamonds. By being so exclusive, Birkin became a must-have accessory for celebrities (Tonello 2009).

How does Hermes determine the price for their bag? Normally, we determine a price for a product by comparing it with similar products. For example, while at a farmer's market you see that most producers charge $1 for a pound of apples. As you wander amongst the many fruit sellers, you discover one stall that is selling what appear to be higher quality apples for $2 per pound. You also know that apples normally range in price from $1 to $2 depending on the type, quality, and season.

Figure 7.1   Birkin bag
Source: Theorb, Wikipedia.

Now you can compare the $1 and $2 apples and decide whether the difference in quality, type, etc., makes it worthwhile to pay an extra $1. In your analysis, you leave out supply and demand, net present value or expected value; you just use a mental shortcut by comparing the prices of apples with a reference point. This is a simple and effective analytical process. In the case of Birkin bags, the situation is not so simple. There are no readily available reference points to help determine what the cost should be for a Birkin bag. Therefore, Hermes is free to ask for any price when they first introduce the bag and, at that point, the price becomes the anchor that will be used to determine the prices of all Birkin bags. People commonly rely on anchors, or one particular piece of information or reference point to make decisions. If this anchor is set up incorrectly or arbitrarily, it may lead to wrong decisions. This effect is called the *anchoring heuristic* (Tversky and Kahneman 1974).

Here is another example. In 1993, federal regulators forced public companies to disclose their compensation to senior management, which at that time was 131 times as much as the average worker. In 2008, the average CEO's combined compensation was 369 times greater than the average worker (Ariely 2009). The underlying reason for such growth is the anchoring heuristic. After CEO compensation started to be disclosed, every board began comparing the salary of their CEO and others in a similar position, which might not be the correct reference or anchor point to use. Remember, the main argument for enormous CEO salaries is that other CEOs have a similar level of compensation. Obviously, boards do not want a bad CEO: so they find the "normal" compensation in their industry and add 10–30% to attract the best candidates.

Anchoring often manifests itself in estimation of project costs, resources, or duration. For example, we estimate that a project would take 20 days based on experience with a similar project, but this reference point may not be applicable to the current project. Now, even if we add contingency time to perform probabilistic analysis (e.g. 15 to 25 days' duration), the result will still be incorrect.

Here is another outcome related to anchoring. Project managers often compare project performance against benchmarks. In many cases this is a good practice; however, incorrect benchmarks can give incorrect insights into the actual performance of projects. For example, a project manager may discover that administrative costs for the similar project were around 10% of the project cost. With this in mind, he or she may start to reduce the project's administration expenses without a clear idea of how administrative expenses for the previous project were calculated and whether these numbers are applicable for this specific case.

Another bias related to anchoring is called the *focusing effect* (Schkade and Kahneman 1998). The focusing effect occurs when decision-makers place too much importance on one aspect of an event or process. Here is a question for you: do you think the senior manager of your company has a good life? If you focus solely on your manager's salary and perks, the answer may be yes. However, you might not know that the manager has a wife and two teenage daughters who spend thousands on perfume, a very critical live-in mother-in-law, a leaky basement, and a slipped disk. He may be a very unhappy man for reasons that have nothing to do with his employment.

The problem with the anchoring heuristic is that it is very difficult to overcome. One suggestion is to use more than one reference point during your analysis of an issue. When you buy a Dooney & Bourke bag, try to assess prices using not just Gucci as a reference, but also bags that you can find at Wal-Mart. When you think about project cost, use more than one as a reference.

Representativeness and Stereotypes

Take a look at Figure 7.2 where this ski resort is located: Aspen, Chamonix, or Whistler? In fact, it is a ski resort in Dizin, north of Tehran. What, a ski resort in Iran, you say? In fact, your reaction would probably be shared with the majority of people who read this book – perhaps because there are no plans to translate this to Persian, but most likely because most of us associate Iran with a warm climate. Also, when we think about Iran, we always recall pictures associated with some political events rather than snowboarding. Therefore, in our minds, we have categorized Iran as a warm place; warm places do not have ski resorts, so the idea that the picture was taken in Iran would not occur to most of us. We made an incorrect decision because we place Iran in a very narrow category.

We like to organize information so it is easy to understand: we create classifications, hierarchies, assign attributes to almost everything we encounter. In most cases this strategy works very well and is an efficient analytical technique.

Figure 7.2   Where is this ski resort located?
Source: Emesik, Wikipedia.

The problem occurs if we incorrectly categorize information and judgments that are based not on the real properties of the thing (object, person, or a process), but rather on the properties of the category or group to which we have assigned it. This is the mistake we made when we passed judgment on the Iranian ski resort.

Remember that most objects are hard to classify. Moreover, people are often uncomfortable with how certain goods or things are categorized. For example, to what type of categories should vehicles like the Mercedes-Benz R-Class belong (Figure 7.3)? Daimler markets it as a multi-purpose vehicle (MPV), but for most people it is a station wagon on anabolic steroids. Without a doubt it is a good family vehicle but, partially because it is hard to classify, sales of the R-class were sluggish (Mercedes-Benz USA 2010).

Cars are not the only things we tend to classify. We tend to classify pretty well everything that we happen across, including people. In our minds, we create certain categories and when we meet people who have certain attributes we try to fit them into these categories, though sometimes it has the same result as trying to fit a square peg into a round hole. Captain Holly Graf was a commander of the Japan-based guided missile cruiser U.S.S. Cowpens (Thompson 2010).

Figure 7.3   Mercedes-Benz R-Class
Source: Wikipedia.

She had all the attributes to place her in the commander category: she was very knowledgeable, experienced, outspoken, and decisive – all necessary attributes when commanding a large navy ship. Because of these attributes, she was promoted into the rank of commander. Unfortunately, people who classified her as a commander type and then promoted her to the position ignored one other important attribute required by leaders: people skills. It turns out Commander Graf had none. After numerous complaints regarding her handling of subordinates and other ranking officers, she was removed from her position as a captain of a billion-dollar warship for "cruelty and maltreatment" of her 400-member crew. According to the Navy inspector general's report and the accounts of officers who served under her command, Holly Graf was the closest thing the U.S. Navy had to a female Captain Bligh. The inspector general's report stated that she repeatedly verbally abused and assaulted her crew.

Our mistakes in classification lead us to create stereotypes or develop prejudices. For example, we may classify suppliers from small companies as generally unreliable and low quality. While this may be true in some cases, it is also true that because of these prejudices we may ignore good suppliers and overpay large companies that may also have problems with quality. We often judge people skills based on the job title or job description. For example, project managers often think that software engineers may not be able to work with clients because it is not part of their job description. As a result, they hire business analysts to perform tasks that most software engineers could do just as well.

But here is a much less trivial consequence of our attempt to classify things. People make judgments about probabilities and risks based on the category that this object, person, or process represents. This heuristic is called *representativeness*. Representativeness can lead to a number of mental mistakes. Take a look at Question 4 of our judgment test. The probability of the three events occurring together (in "conjunction") is always less than or equal to the probability of either one occurring alone. Therefore, the more detailed description, such as "the exterminator was a big guy in a black suit and sunglasses, who spoke with a Russian accent," is less probable (Figure 7.4). This effect is called the *conjunction fallacy* (Tversky and Kahneman 1983).

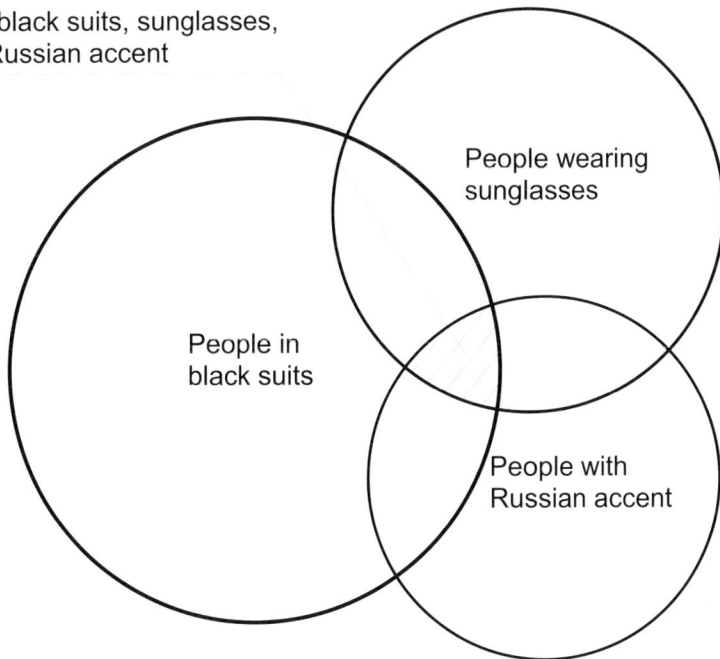

Figure 7.4   Conjunction fallacy

Here is another effect related to representativeness heuristic. Take a look at Question 11 from our judgment test. This effect is called *ignoring regression to mean* – the tendency to expect extreme events to be followed by similar extreme events. Let us imagine that your team is consistently underestimating the cost of projects. However, two of your latest cost estimations were very accurate. You start to believe that you are now on a winning streak. The reality is that unless the quality of your project management has mysteriously improved or you have a new process that is expected to improve your forecasts, you should not expect to change your chances that all future project cost estimation will be accurate. A similar situation can occur if you suddenly experience a sudden growth in your investment: a 10% return for the last quarter after 6% for the past few years. Time to buy that vacation home, right? No, unfortunately, we have to disappoint you: 10% is probably an aberration.

To mitigate the negative effect of representativeness, try to think about different methods to categorize objects or events. For example, you have to estimate how long it would take to develop a software user interface. This particular task could belong to different categories:

- user interface development

- development using a particular tool

- capabilities of a particular programmer or particular team.

By approaching this task from multiple viewpoints, you can make your estimates based on similar projects for each different category.

Some Other Heuristics and Biases

The list of heuristics biases is quite extensive. For the sake of brevity, we have provided a list of biases that are most common in project management, some of which we have already discussed in previous chapters.

CONFIRMATION BIAS

People tend to confirm preconceptions or hypotheses, independent of whether they are true or not. We learned about this bias in Chapter 2.

IGNORING BASE RATE FREQUENCIES

People assess the probability of something based on evidence without taking sufficient account of the "base rate" or "prior probability" of the evidence. We will learn about zero-risk bias in Chapter 13.

ILLUSION OF CONTROL

People often believe that they are in control of a situation; although, in reality, they are not. You have probably heard about telekinesis, or the direct influence of the mind on a physical system, in which a system or object is manipulated in a way that cannot be entirely accounted for by the mediation of any known physical energy: bending spoons, moving objects. Many instances of telekinesis can be attributed to the illusion of control (Bösch et al. 2006). Similar to mediums and other participants in paranormal activities, project managers often believe that they are in control of situations when in reality they are not.

OMISSION BIAS

People have a tendency to judge harmful actions as worse than equally harmful omissions. What would be better: to observe a potential problem in a project and do nothing or actually be part of the problem? The result will be the same: the project will be behind schedule. This bias often manifests itself when people are making decisions regarding safety and security. People sometimes think that the result of not reporting a potential safety violation is not as bad as actually breaking safety rules.

OPTIMISM BIAS OR PLANNING FALLACY

People tend to be overoptimistic about the outcome of planned actions. We learned about this bias in Chapter 2.

OVERCONFIDENCE

People tend to overestimate the accuracy of their predictions. We learned about this bias in Chapter 2.

PUBLICATION BIAS

People have a tendency to report results that confirm expectations differently from results that are negative or inconclusive. This is a very common phenomenon in research and development projects. Negative results or results which do not confirm the original hypothesis are also valuable and should be reported in the same manner as positive results.

STATUS QUO BIAS

People tend not to change an established behavior unless the incentive to change is compelling. We learn about this bias in Chapter 12.

ZERO-RISK BIAS

Sometimes people feel better if they completely eliminate risk rather than mitigate it. We will learn about zero-risk bias in Chapter 13.

LOSS AVERSION

People tend to strongly prefer avoiding losses versus acquiring gains. We will learn about loss aversion in Chapter 11.

SMART TIPS
- **Availability bias** is a tendency to predict the frequency of an event based on how easily the events can be brought to mind. To mitigate this bias, perform analysis based on as many samples of information as possible.
- **Anchoring:** we rely on a piece of information or "anchor" when making decisions. Try to find multiple reference points or anchors when you are estimating or analyzing something (e.g. cost, duration, resources).
- **Representativeness:** we judge about probability of events based on how well the events resemble available data. Ask yourself a question: is it possible to categorize this event, activity or object differently?

8

What Makes Your Project Team Happy?

Only happy people can fully contribute to a project. In this chapter, we are going to learn what happiness means; in Chapter 14 we will discuss what we can do to make ourselves, our colleagues, and, perhaps most importantly, our bosses happier. Happiness increases when we earn or have something that is better than what we currently have. We become less happy when we lose something that we have spent a long time accumulating or if our expectations are much higher than actual performance or experience. If fact, it is possible to use a test to determine how happy you are at work and in life.

Why Are We Talking About Happiness in Project Management?

You might be wondering why we are talking about happiness if this is supposed to be a book about project management. Researchers reviewed interaction with the type of people who most likely will bring you more happiness. Take a look at Table 8.1 (Baucells and Sarin 2008a).

Table 8.1   Happiness while spending time with different people

	Interactive with	Relative Happiness
1	Friends	3.3
2	Parents and relatives	3.0
3	Spouse	2.8
4	Own children	2.7
5	Co-workers	2.6
6	Clients, customers, etc.	2.4
7	Alone	2.2
8	Boss	2.0

In project management, you are either the boss or you have a boss or, if you are like most of us, you are a bit of both. Can you imagine that according to the above table for your subordinates spending time with you is probably worse than spending time by themselves? This does provide a startling perspective on how you might approach your next conversation with a subordinate. (This is an average, so we hope that it doesn't apply to you.)

Unhappy people do not do a good job. This may seem obvious, but there has been a lot of research on the subject, even going so far as to provide a framework for the collapse of slavery (Staw et al. 1994; Cropanzano and Wright 2001; Baas et al. 2008). Nevertheless, some project managers are under the impression that it is not their responsibility to keep their team members happy; they get paid for their work and that should be enough. This might be the correct attitude for manual labor, which does not require a lot of thought, but in all other projects which require even a little bit of creativity, having an unhappy team and positive results will leave you disappointed in the outcome.

So, if you do not want to be a person with whom your employee would prefer not to spend time with, you probably should learn more about what makes people happy.

Why Did Eliot Spitzer Do It?

Former governor of New York Eliot Spitzer seemed to have it all: as governor of New York he had one of the most coveted political jobs in the country, he had a beautiful wife and kids, and was extremely wealthy. Nevertheless, on March 10, 2008, the *New York Times* reported that Spitzer was a client of a prostitution ring under investigation by the federal government. Two days later, he announced his resignation as governor of New York, effective March 17, citing "private failings" (*Huntington Post* 2008). We can only guess what his motivations were when he requested the services of Ashley Alexandra Dupre, aka "Kristen". But here is a theory about what might have caused him to risk his job, family and reputation for the company of the aforementioned Ashley Dupre. People's level of happiness is directly related to how they perceive their success: are they earning more, have they become more influential, have they met their personal goals? In other words, for us to remain happy, we must always be receiving some increment in money, job, family, or even something smaller like a better car, higher-class hotels, or being able to fly business class (Baucells and Sarin 2008a). But when people start losing something they become extremely frustrated.

> *Increment law: people must always have something better than they had before to feel happier.*

Go back and review Question 5 of our Judgment Test. James Clean the dishwasher is happier than millionaire Ronald Drump because the financial situation of James increased exponentially, while Ronald's wealth was constantly shrinking. People often believe that acquiring huge wealth in a short period time, for example by winning in a lottery, will make them happier. It is a mental error. In most cases, they will only experience a short period of increased happiness until they become accustomed to their new wealth, at which time they will return to their previous levels of happiness, all other things being equal. If they don't properly manage their money, the wealth would start shrinking, and they would become very unhappy.

The tragedy of Eliot Spitzer is that he had reached a point in his life where it was extremely difficult to add any incremental gains to those things – power, prestige, wealth – that he valued. What could he do to keep himself happy? Become president, earn more money, and initiate a massive reform of the New York state government? All of these things would be extremely difficult, so he decided to do something simpler: engage in risky behavior with call girls.

Another phenomenon that affects our happiness is what one of the leading researchers in this area calls accumulation (Baucells and Sarin 2008b). Over time, we accumulate things: family, wealth, job experience, etc. (Figure 8.1). The combination of these "goods" represents our level of happiness. If we lose any of our "goods," we become frustrated. For example, a person could work in an organization for many years, during which their salary increased year over year and the expertise and knowledge of their job accumulates. However, often due to circumstances beyond their control, they are laid off. Their accumulation of goods is significantly diminished, leading them to feel extremely unhappy. However, if after some time they find a new job and are able to quickly surpass their previous accumulations, their level of happiness will also be much higher than it was before. So in the long term, being laid off may not be so bad.

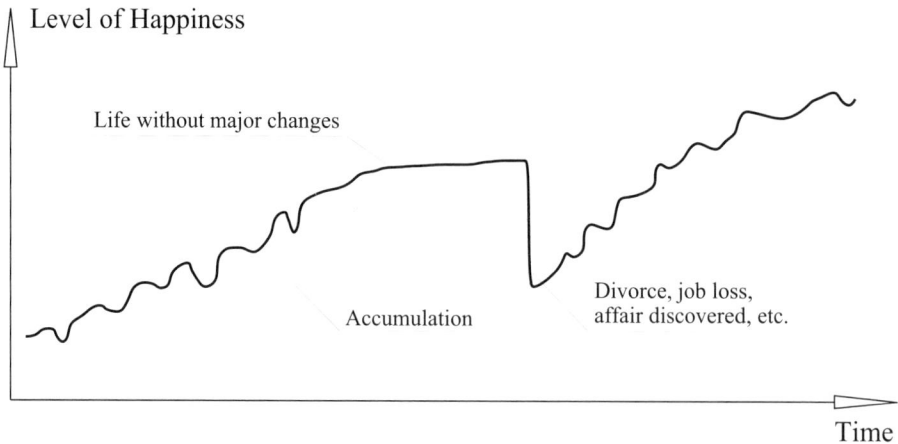

Figure 8.1   Laws of accumulation and increment

> *Accumulation law: people become unhappy if they even insignificantly*
> *lose something which they slowly accumulated before.*

These theories of increment and accumulation seem to explain the irrational behaviors of many celebrities, politicians, or entrepreneurs. At the beginning of their careers actresses, politicians, and business entrepreneurs have some success and move to the top of their profession. But as life will have it, not all goes smoothly, and their careers seem to stall or even decline. The actress sees her plum roles disappear, the politician feels frustrated stuck in a legislative body without an apparent path upwards, or the entrepreneur's latest venture fails to meet expectations. Faced with these obstacles they may try to maintain their previous increments through what seems to be irrational behaviors: drugs, affairs, or shady business dealings. Unfortunately, this usually ends up in scandal, they lose accumulations and everything becomes worse than before.

If you are not a celebrity but simply a lowly project manager or project team member who is flying below the radar of the popular media, it does not mean that you are immune from problems related to increment and accumulation. But in most cases these problems manifest themselves differently. If your salary increase barely covers inflation, you don't learn anything new, you don't get additional responsibility for years, or don't get any recognition for your work, you stop doing anything productive. Regardless of how enthusiastic you were at the beginning of your career, if you don't receive increments and accumulation, you will become unattached to your project and your job. As a result, organizations lose the ability to produce high-quality, innovative projects at a reasonable cost.

Australian researchers even managed to put a dollar figure on the law of increment and accumulation (Martin 2009). They asked people to describe how satisfied they were with their lives on a scale of 0 to 10. Most Australians gave themselves an eight; however, this number could change if the subject has just experienced a major life event or anticipated one. After completing the survey, researchers performed some calculations, similar to those that we will describe in Chapter 10, and put dollar figures to the major life events (Table 8.2).

Table 8.2   Dollar figures associated with life events

	Life Event	Woman	Man
1	Marriage	$15,600	$31,600
2	Birth of child	$8,700	$32,600
3	Separation	–$8,900	–$109,300
4	Death of loved one	–$130,900	–$627,300
5	Illness	–$50,300	–$360,000
6	Moving home	$2,600	–$16,000
Average salary in Australia in 2007 (Bourlioufas 2007)		$51,000	$61,000

It is not surprising that men and women would have different perceptions of these major life events. For example, if women feel somewhat happy about moving, men are somewhat less enthusiastic about the prospect. Marriage seems to provide a very strong increment in our lives. Separation or divorce has a significantly larger effect on men compared with women. Compare these numbers with the average salary in Australia. For men, marriage is equivalent to the average yearly salary: divorce is the equivalent to just over four years' salary. This makes for a bad formula for men, as they would have to marry four times to regain the loss of accumulation that they would experience from a single divorce. An area where people can provide themselves with a constant increment without risking too much is children. Ten children will provide happiness that is equivalent to five years' salary for a man and 1.7 years' salary for a woman. Perhaps this discrepancy is due to the fact that in a family of 10 children, the man is able to get relief from the mob at work, while mothers tend to bear the greatest burden of child-rearing. This research does not include events at work, but we can assume that positive events at work, such as completion of a successful project and receiving appropriate recognition, would have at least a three-digit dollar figure behind it.

Why Some People Are Happier Than Others

Behavioral geneticist David T. Lykken studied identical twins for many years. He found that about half of your happiness depends on your genes. He based this finding on a study of identical twins whose happiness is correlated by 50% even when they grow up in different houses (Lykken and Tellegen 1996). About 10% is the result of various measurable life circumstances, such as socioeconomic status, marital status, health, income, sex, and others. The remaining 40% is a combination of unknown factors and the results of actions that individuals deliberately engage in to become happier (Lyubomirsky et al. 2005).

Happiness also depends on age. Here is an interesting observation: older Americans are generally happier than younger ones. While older people obviously reported more health problems, they reported fewer problems overall. Young adults reported more problems, including troubled relationships, financial issues, and stress at work (Vedantam 2008).

Human relationships are consistently found to be the most important factor affecting happiness. According to recent research, happiness in social networks including project teams may spread from person to person (Fowler and Christakis 2009). Researchers followed nearly 5,000 individuals for 20 years and found that happiness tended to spread through close relationships such as friends, siblings, spouses, next-door neighbors, and co-workers. More encouraging news: happiness spreads more consistently through social networks than unhappiness. Moreover, the structure of the social network appears to have an impact on happiness, as people who were very central (with many friends and friends of friends) were significantly more likely to be happy than those on the periphery of the network. The implication is that happiness can spread through a population like a virus. Now you can see why it is important to create a "happy" environment at work, particularly in your project team: you can "infect" many other people with happiness.

If happiness spreads in a project team like a virus and older people tend to be generally happier than younger ones, it would be reasonable to assume that if you have a mixed-age project team, it will be happier than a younger project team. The "happiness" virus from older team members will spread to younger people, while the "unhappiness" virus from younger members could come to dominate your team's morale (Figure 8.2).

Figure 8.2   Spreading the virus of happiness
Source: iStockPhoto, Alex Alexeev.

Habituation

Habituation is the psychological process in which there is a decreased response to a stimulus after repeated exposure to that stimulus over a duration of time.

Here is a common scenario. After years of hard work you have saved enough money to build a large new home in an upscale neighborhood. Construction takes about a year and you move into your dream home. For a few months you feel quite elated: however, this initial elation subsides over the next few months and, after a while, you have returned to the same level that you had prior to moving into the house. You will still enjoy your new house, but not as much as when you first moved in. Move on a few years: you are now completely used to your new home; it is nice and convenient, but you feel that there isn't anything really special about it. After a few more years you begin to think about building an even bigger and better home. What has happened to you is called *habituation* (Gilbert 2006). When people get familiar with a routine or something else, the pleasure that they derive from it diminishes the more familiar they become with it over time. Habituation is one of the fundamental mechanisms behind the law of increment, which we discussed previously; unfortunately, it commonly afflicts members of project teams. When somebody is required to do the same tasks over and over again, he or she may lose interest and motivation, regardless of how interesting the job may appear.

Why Time Seems to Pass More Quickly as We Age

Have you ever noticed that as you age, time appears to go past more quickly? When we attended school, we hoped that the time until we graduated would pass as quickly as possible and time seemed to move extremely slowly. As we move into middle age and beyond, life seems to pass by much more quickly, and we dream of ways to make it slow down.

There are a number of theories regarding this phenomenon: one suggests our brain is wired to analyze and accumulate new experiences. When we are young, our brains are absorbing vast amounts of new experiences and information, observing new things and having new interactions. During childhood, we process so many more new experiences and specific incidents it affects our perception of time and the passage of time appears to be slower. However, as we age, we have fewer "new" experiences. As we get older, our brain categorizes similar experiences into groups and we remember fewer instances of them, so time seems to pass faster.

You probably have vivid memories of your graduation, your wedding, the birth of your child, and other unique and rare events. At the same time, you have trouble remembering what happened at work last Wednesday. It was just like hundreds of other Wednesdays at work that you have experienced. Your brain "skips" it as a common experience.

To stay happy we need to have more unique and memorable moments so that they are grouped in our brain with something else. It is possible to create these moments at work, where we spend a significant portion of our life, so we would not feel the accelerated pace of life and become happier.

Managing Exceptions

Here is another interesting phenomenon. *It is often better to think about possessing something than actually possessing it.* You can dream about becoming a project manager for three years. Then you finally become a manager and are in charge of a medium-sized project with five people on your project team. You find that although you are enjoying yourself, it is not quite as enjoyable as when you first started thinking about it. In general our imagination fails to realize that situations will feel differently once they actually happen. You may worry about passing an exam when you are preparing for it, but during the exam you don't feel as bad as you thought you would.

When people think about events that have not yet occurred, their imaginations use memories of previous events to create or invent a possible scenario. These imaginations can be quite different from reality. If your expectations are significantly different from your real experience, you may feel unhappy or vice versa. In the movie *Christmas Vacation* (1989), Clark Griswold (Chevy Chase) imagines how he is going to spend his Christmas bonus: he wants to build a swimming pool in his backyard. In his imaginary swimming pool, he placed a beautiful young lady based on his memory of a department store clerk. So when Clark's boss decided to save money and Clark did not receive his Christmas bonus, he was understandably unhappy. As these movies go, it ended badly, with the boss being taken hostage by Clark's semi-lunatic cousin Eddie Johnson (Randy Quaid).

When we work on a project, we have expectations that the project will be successful, customers will be satisfied, management will be happy, and we will be properly compensated. These expectations are products of our imagination based on our previous experiences directly or indirectly related to the project. If there is a discrepancy between our expectations and reality, we may become unhappy. This will affect our memory and, therefore, expectations for future projects. Because of this, it is very important that we manage expectations as part of project management.

How Happy Are You in Your Project Team?

Would you like to measure your level of happiness? There are a number of tests that can help you if you are so inclined (Hills and Argyle 2002; Francis1999; Pavot and Diener 1993). There has been some criticism of these tests, arguing that they do not accurately gauge the level of happiness (Kashdan 2004). Nevertheless, we have decided to include our version of a happiness test (Table 8.3). To answer each question, circle the appropriate number and sum the results of your answers.

Table 8.3   Test your happiness

		Strongly Disagree	Somewhat Disagree	Neutral	Somewhat Agree	Strongly Agree
1	I am intensely interested in my colleagues.	1	2	3	4	5
2	My boss is a good person.	1	2	3	5	5
3	I don't think I am a good fit with this project team.	5	4	3	2	1
4	I apply a lot of energy to these projects.	1	2	3	4	5
5	I like to work on my project: I find it very rewarding.	1	2	3	4	5
6	I don't have particularly happy memories about previous events in my team.	5	4	3	2	1
7	I don't find it easy to make decisions.	5	4	3	2	1
8	There is a gap between what I would like to do and what I am doing in this team.	5	4	3	2	1
9	I am very satisfied with my job.	1	2	3	4	5
10	I am not very optimistic about my career in this organization.	5	4	3	2	1
11	I can find time for most home activities even when I am busy at work.	1	2	3	4	5
12	I usually have a positive influence on decisions in my project team.	1	2	3	4	5
13	My project team values my opinion.	1	2	3	4	5
14	I laugh a lot at work.	1	2	3	4	5
15	Almost all my co-workers are very good people. I have very warm feelings towards them.	1	2	3	4	5
16	At work I feel fully mentally alert, committed and involved.	1	2	3	4	5
17	When I work I often experience joy and elation.	1	2	3	4	5
18	I do not know why I have stayed with this company for so long.	5	4	3	2	1
19	I don't have fun interacting with other people in our team.	5	4	3	2	1
20	I don't think the company I'm working for is a good one.	5	4	3	2	1

This test was not designed to compare yourself with other people; instead, we recommend that you take this test several times during the course of a project and compare how your reported levels of happiness change over time. Just so you can determine where you stand in regards to the greater population, the average score is 60. If your score is below 25 – you may be having a particularly bad day. Perhaps your boss was not in a good mood today. Take the test again tomorrow to see if you improve; if not, you should probably think about updating your résumé. If your score is greater than 110, you may have a problem as well: you are too happy. Take a break, and when you have sobered up, take it again.

SMART TIPS
- Unhappy people don't perform at their best. As a project manager, making your team happy should be one of your first priorities.
- To be happy, always try to get something more compared with what you had before. This "more" is not necessarily a monetary increase.
- Try to manage your project expectations: discrepancies between your expectations and actual events will make you and your team unhappy.

PART III

Project Analysis vs. Mental Errors

9

How to Process Project Information

In Part II of this book we learned about common memory errors which we have to deal with in our ordinary life and in project management in particular. As we saw, there are many situations that can cause illusions which can lead to very costly errors. Now we will learn how to analyze information and mitigate potential mental problems, particularly how to process the huge amounts of information we receive on a daily basis. For example, not all of the information we receive is of the highest quality; in fact, much of the information we receive is deliberately manipulated to "trick" our brains, so that we make decisions that may not be in our best interests, like buying something that we do not want or even need. In this chapter we will learn how to analyze information to avoid illusions and make better choices.

My Dentist Has a Very Nice Website

Imagine that you are managing the development of a software application for the computer-aided design of bridges and interchanges. As one of the requirements, your team needs to implement an interactive map of the bridges and roads. Obviously, you don't want to develop your own mapping engine from scratch, so decided to purchase a mapping component for your software. There are dozens of such components available. Some of them are freeware; others cost a lot of money. Some of them support multiple mapping data formats; others work only with one proprietary format. Some of them work for desktop computers; others have a web interface. It will take a while to formulate selection criteria; then you will need to evaluate the different applications, possibly by contacting different vendors. Then you will need to get different quotes, procure the software, and get training. Underlying all of this is a fundamental issue: you need to process a huge amount of information.

Figure 9.1   How to choose a dentist
Source: Alex Alexeev.

It is not enough to simply cruise the Internet and make your decision purely on what you discover on the websites of various vendors, just as you should not select your dentist based solely on the dentist's website (Figure 9.1) as they tend to be somewhat self-serving. But remember, the mapping component is only 1% of your project. How long should the software selection and procurement take? How much will it all cost, including evaluation, training, and software licenses? Most likely, you will only develop very rough estimates.

This is a key issue in project management. As part of your job as a project manager, you have to process a lot of information: you must deal with the demands of numerous stakeholders, complex technologies, conflicting requirements, and ensuring that all of this is accomplished within a short period of time. To properly process this information you have to do some analysis, but you cannot spend all of your time selecting suppliers or calculating your budget. How can you process this mass of information quickly and efficiently? Where can you take shortcuts and where would taking shortcuts lead to problems?

All Marketers Are Liars

Car manufacturers spend more than $13 billion a year on advertising their products. According to Jeffrey Hauser, sales consultant and author of *Inside the Yellow Pages* (Hauser 2007), auto manufacturers usually spend about 1% of their revenues on advertising. Figures for other industries are much higher: retail stores: 2% to 3%, service businesses: 3% to 5%, new business startups: 5% to 7%, fast-moving consumer products: 8% to 10%, pharmaceutical or cosmetic companies: 20% and up (Hauser 2010). Eventually, the cost of this advertising is passed onto consumers as part of the final price. This means that when you buy a $30,000 automobile, you are paying the advertising companies a few hundred dollars for their effort in persuading you to purchase the product. If this were the planet Vulcan as fictionalized in the *Star Trek* series, where the inhabitants are governed completely by logic and rational thought, they would select a car by reading the analysis provided by such publications as *Consumer Reports*, which includes unbiased comparisons of all the models with prices, features, reliability, etc. But we are not Vulcans and businesses realize that they can push the odds that we will buy their particular product in their favor by appealing to our emotions. So they spend billions to appeal to your emotions and try to minimize the effect that reason will play in your buying decisions. In effect, they are making an appeal to the irrational side of your nature to part with your hard-earned cash to purchase something that you probably do not need. Undercoating anyone? So let us be clear regarding what we are saying: the next time you purchase a new car, you will pay hundreds of dollars extra for someone's deliberate attempt to delude you. A red sports car will not make your hair grow back, nor will a large pickup turn you into a cowboy.

It is not our intent to argue that all advertising is irrational. It certainly is not from the perspective of the manufacturers. Advertising is a multi-billion-dollar industry that provides a valuable service. How would you be able to notify people about your new invention, or the massive 50% sale off all furniture that you are having this weekend (though in reality it still represents about a 20% markup)?

Another interesting phenomenon contributing to the irrational choices is the cost of brands. If you buy a Coca-Cola drink, you are paying a premium for the brand. According to the MillwardBrown Optimor Ranking, in 2007 the most expensive brands were Google ($66.4 billion), General Electric ($61.9 billion), and Microsoft ($55 billion) (MillwardBrown 2011). It is true that often brand-name products are superior to the less expensive alternatives. But often when a similar, but less costly, alternative is available, people will still choose to purchase a brand-name product. For example, generally the only difference between brand-name and generic prescription drugs is price. According to Blue Cross Insurance, Prozac is 19 times more expensive than its generic equivalent, Zantac 16.5 times more expensive, and Ritalin is 2.5 times more expensive (Blue Cross and Blue Shield of Michigan 2010). Obviously, when it comes to particular brand-name products, people are under some kind of illusion. Why else would they pay 19 times more for the exact same substance just because it carries a certain brand name? At least when you wear a Rolex watch this sends out a message about yourself – that you are wealthy and can afford it. Unless you are willing to open up your bathroom cabinet for the perusal of friends and strangers to prove that you can afford to needlessly spend money on brand-name drugs, spending that extra money does not convey any concrete benefits.

Seth Godin, who wrote the bestselling book *All Marketers Are Liars*, noticed that successful marketers don't talk about features or even benefits of a product. Instead, they convey a story that people want to believe (Godin 2005). They tell us that a $40,000 Lexus ES would be much better than a $25,000 Toyota Camry, though they are virtually the same car, that a brand-name drug is more effective than a generic, though they are exactly the same product. Advertisers have a repertoire of tricks to convince us to make irrational choices. They appeal to our emotions, use available and anchoring heuristics, trick our memory, and use all sorts of other sleights of hand that we reviewed in Part II of this book.

When you process information for your project, be aware that many people want you to make a choice that may be beneficial for them, but not for you. It is not only marketers that want you to make mental mistakes. Intentionally or unintentionally, our managers and our team members, our government and our media, our customers and our suppliers create a breeding ground for us to make irrational choices by supplying us with distorted, incomplete, and improperly analyzed information. The world is very dangerous: there is no such thing as 100% reliable and unbiased information. All information we receive has to some extent been transformed by the source it came from. This transformed or processed information most likely, intentionally or unintentionally, includes someone's personal bias, which may impair your ability to make good decisions.

"Time Zone" Trick in Project Management?

In 2010, the Canadian government proposed to change the lyrics of the Canadian national anthem from "true patriot love in all thy sons command" to the perhaps quite cumbersome "thou dost in us command" to make it gender neutral (*CTV News* 2010). Revamping the Canadian anthem to meet some amorphous "inclusivity" objective turned out to be very low on the list of priorities of most people and this initiative was quickly dropped from the government's agenda.

The Russian government had an even more revolutionary proposal that also had negligible correlation with the necessities of the country: they wanted to reduce the number of time zones across the country to somehow magically improve the nation's economy. In fact, time zone changes occur quite frequently in Russia compared with other countries. In most cases, the changes only affect specific regions that are forced to move back and forth from one time zone to another. Within governments or other organization, schemes such as this are quite common when leaders are faced with many intractable problems such as unemployment, the economy, regional or political disputes. They invent an issue in the hopes of distracting people from the more pressing issues at hand. If people are really upset about job losses, lack of services, taxes, propose a time zone change or the date for switching to Daylight Saving Time. In the short term, people will be more concerned about getting to work on time and will forget that the government just raised taxes. Once people become habituated to the time zone change, the government has an arsenal of other potential innovations: start major discussions in regards to changing the colors of the national coat of arms, reintroduce a new format for license plates, or change the regulations related to passport photos for babies (no smiling).

Experienced project managers know about the "time zone" trick. If senior management asks about something they cannot deliver, project managers will focus the presentation on something small and perhaps irrelevant that everybody understands and that can be delivered quite quickly. The project is behind schedule. This fact can be mentioned briefly, but it's much better to focus on things such as a successful client presentation or the results of the latest fire drill. By switching attention from the poor project performance to the exciting, but essentially irrelevant, events, we can create the illusion that the project delay is not all that important.

Do you want your software development project to be approved? No problem. Just briefly explain the project in terms that no one else in the room understands and then demonstrate a marketing brochure with a portrait of Lady Gaga. The brochure and the appropriateness of Lady Gaga would be discussed for an hour and your project will be approved without any unnecessary questions.

"Peak-end" Rule in Project Management

Here is another illusion related to the way people process information. In a test, one group of patients had a standard colonoscopy. In a second group, after a standard colonoscopy, the doctor left the instrument in place for a short time. It was unpleasant but not as much as for the first group because the instrument was not moving. It turned out that over a five-year period after the exam, patients in the second group were more likely to comply with calls for follow-up colonoscopies than patients in the first group. The reason was that people in the second group had a much less unpleasant experience at the end of the procedure (Schwartz 2005). This effect, how we judge our past experiences – almost entirely on how they were at their peak (whether pleasant or unpleasant) and how they ended – is called the "peak-end" rule (Kahneman 1999). In fact the "peak-end" rule may be an instance of the representativeness heuristic, which we discussed in Chapter 7.

According to this rule, in theory you can tell your boss exactly what you think about the organization, project, or about him personally, as long as at the end of the conversation you tell him that he is a great visionary and superb leader. However, we strongly recommend that you do not experiment with this, as in particular situations it may not unfold as planned and your boss will remember all of your opinions with negative consequences for you.

Filtering Information for Your Project

Take a look at Question 6 from our Judgment Test. If you did not read Dr. Mara Sidoli's paper "Farting as a Defense against Unspeakable Dread," the title would sound quite … how to say it politely … very strange. But in reality it is valuable research published in a peer-reviewed journal.

Not all things which seem to be strange are actually irrational (Ig Nobel 2010). Here are a few examples. The Ig Nobel Prizes are a parody of the Nobel Prizes given for 10 achievements that "first make people laugh, and then make them think." Francis M. Fesmire of the University of Tennessee's College of Medicine received the 2006 Ig Nobel Award in Medicine for his paper "Termination of Intractable Hiccups with Digital Rectal Massage." Claire Rind and Peter Simmons of Newcastle University, in the U.K., received their 2005 Ig Nobel Peace Prize for electrically monitoring the activity of a brain cell in a locust while that locust was watching selected highlights from the movie *Star Wars*. At first glance, performing research on locusts watching *Star Wars* or treating hiccups through unconventional methods can seem a waste of time. However, taken in another light, these pursuits do make sense and represent quite valuable research.

Since there is only a limited amount of information that we can process, the first thing we do is dismiss information that we deem irrelevant. This approach works quite well in most cases. The question is how should people decide what is relevant and what is not. We recommend that for each problem you have, you should clearly define a set of filters for selecting relevant information. For example, if you are trying to book a hotel in Las Vegas using the Internet, you can start with a very broad set of criteria, such as hotel ratings, location, and amenities. When you see the results, you can narrow your search based on information from the previous search and continue to do so until you find what you are looking for. If you use a very narrow set of filters at the beginning, such as hotels on the strip, you may miss good deals for hotels in the downtown area.

For example, if you are trying to choose a mapping component for your bridge and interchange design software, you need to create a comprehensive list of 40 applications and then apply the following filters:

- remove all that are not web based: this will remove 50% of the candidates from your list

- remove all that do not support a standard mapping data format: this will remove another 25% from your original list

- remove all that cost more than $25 per license: this will leave you with a final list of eight candidates.

Now you may have only eight software applications. You may now use a checklist to compare features of different software tools. Interestingly, among these eight applications there are some innovative tools; for example, some are optimized for smartphones and tablet computers – something that you did not consider when you were creating your selection criteria. Since you have already removed 32 applications from you candidate list which were obviously irrelevant, you can now spend some time reviewing some innovative tools.

I Did Not Read This Book, But I Know I Do Not Like It

"I don't understand why people like Placido Domingo's singing: he coughs, forgets the words, and cannot sing half the notes."

"Have you ever heard Placido Domingo sing?"

"Not in person, but my neighbor Joe sings all of Placido's songs in the shower."

Unfortunately, we hear or participate in similar exchanges all the time, though they may not have as good a punch line. When we are asked to express an opinion about something that we have little or no expertise in, we generally respond without too much hesitation. Here is another example. In 1957 Boris Pasternak wrote his novel *Doctor Zhivago* (Pasternak 1997). For his efforts, Pasternak was awarded the Nobel Prize for Literature in 1958 (which he refused to accept). The book was frowned upon by the Soviet authorities, but had great success in Western countries. Because of *Doctor Zhivago's* success in the West, Russian authorities ran a campaign against the book. In published letters and during meetings it was very common to hear the following opinion, "I did not read *Doctor Zhivago*, but strongly condemn it." How could people read the book if it was prohibited? Later on this phrase became an adage in Russian culture, which people used when forced to give an opinion on a subject of which they had little or no knowledge. As an aside, we hope "I did not read this book but I strongly condemn it" isn't heard when discussing this book.

People tend to express opinion when they are asked even if they are not familiar with the subject or did not perform the analysis.

Why do we feel compelled to provide an opinion on something of which we know little or nothing? Psychologically, there is the fear of embarrassment, of being seen as being out of the loop or uninformed.

Let's assume that you read the following headline: "Florida state budget fails to account for snow removal in Florida Keys." Or an opposition politician on TV paints a vivid picture of the horrible consequences for residents if Florida experiences its first snowfall in living memory. Once you are exposed to this, you most likely will form an opinion. The politician may have a good point or not (we refuse comment on these matters so as not to influence your opinion). However, the main issue is just that, once your opinion is formed, it not only shapes your own actions; it will serve to shape the opinion of anyone you discuss this with. You can actually express opinion indirectly or passively merely by viewing it on the Internet, as web traffic influences how some websites work. The more times you view the webpage, the higher the ranking the page will receive and will increase the spread of this information. If you tend to side with the politician regarding the snowfall budget, your point of view will tend to spread to other people. We don't blame you. The tendency to express opinions when asked is a psychological effect that we all inherited from our early ancestors. We place the blame on individuals or organizations (government, media, polling companies, marketers, etc.) who insist on soliciting opinions from people on very complex subjects who have little or no knowledge on the subject.

This effect is very common in project management. How long does it take to create a report? Often, we can be inclined to come up with an answer right on the spot to avoid being seen as either incompetent or uninformed. It is better to ask for additional time to analyze the question as a wrong answer can have a life of its own and lead to all sorts of unexpected difficulties.

Any Suggestions About What to Do?

So at this point you might be saying (and we hope that you are at least thinking this), "You've convinced me: yes, there is lots of bad information out there, information is distorted, important components are missing, and we cannot even have complete trust in reputable sources of information. But I have a project to manage. What should I do?"

Here are a few ideas:

1.   To judge the quality of project information, try to understand how
      this information was obtained. In particular, how many layers of
      interpreters are between you and the original source of information?
      Was it a result of detailed analysis or was it just a judgment call of
      one individual?

2.   Even if the project information comes from very reputable sources,
      try to understand how well substantiated it is and what is the
      original source of information. Could you find any original project
      documents: plans, notes, design documents?

3.   When selecting product, services, and components for your project,
      you will be approached by people who will distort information
      in an attempt to sell you something. Ideally, you should perform
      a competitive analysis of features and benefits of products you
      are looking for. However, time constraints may not allow this.
      Therefore, we suggest that before you talk with a salesperson or
      engineer, clearly identify your requirements and record them for
      easy review. Since an analysis of products and services may involve
      a large number of variables, keep the number of questions you ask
      a vendor to a minimum and then steer your conversation towards
      these questions. Otherwise, the vendor may focus on something
      you do not need.

4.   We often dismiss or overlook important information because
      it is new, strange, or does not fit the boundary of your research.
      Always keep an open mind and you might find something from
      a completely different subject area that will improve your project.

5.   If you are asked to provide an opinion (e.g. estimate), always state
      that you will provide one only after a detailed analysis.

6.   Try not to be emotional when processing information. This is
      what has happened with many people during the 2009–10 health
      care reform debates in the U.S. Public health management is such
      a complex issue that experts who have studied the subject their
      entire working lives cannot agree about the consequences of
      particular aspects of the legislation. Nevertheless, people created
      very strong opinions about the subject with subsequent volatile
      emotions. Because the situation became so emotional, people

became very focused and stopped processing new information and the confirmation bias, which we reviewed in Chapter 2, becomes very pervasive. The more emotional people become, the stronger opinions they have and vice versa. To stop this vicious cycle, they have to take a break and completely stop thinking about the issue for some time. Take a deep breath and do the analysis.

7. It takes some effort to obtain and process information. In decision analysis theory, these efforts are called "value of information." In most cases there is an actual cost associated with value of information. If you need to confirm that information you already have is accurate and reliable, you may try to obtain additional data. For example, you may ask a different doctor for a second opinion. Additional information may cost you extra and in many cases it would be cheaper to assume the risk and live with less reliable data than pay for new information. There are a number of formal methods to calculate value of information (Virine and Trumper 2007; Schuyler 2001; Clemen 1996). But you can do a very simple assessment: how much will it cost you to get the additional data; for example, how much time and money will it cost you to go to the second doctor?

SMART TIPS
- Always identify the source of project information; make sure that the information was obtained from detailed analysis or from a knowledgeable neutral expert.
- Before using project information, analyze how relevant the information is to the current project.
- Try not to express your opinion unless you analyzed the issue and are comfortable with your answer; otherwise, you may contribute to the spread of inaccurate information.

10

An Expected Value Manifesto

There are so many analytical techniques and tools, some of which are very complex and require a lot of effort to perform and others which are very industry specific. Because a full survey of all of these tools and techniques could fill an entire encyclopedia, with this book we decided to concentrate on only a few very simple techniques that can provide project managers the most benefit without requiring them to become experts in the field. One of them is expected value analysis. This analysis is a choice engineering method, which means that it is more of a mental exercise rather than a strict and formal project management process. At the same time, going through the expected value thinking process may significantly improve the quality of decisions.

How to Win a Lottery

Questions regarding lotteries are pretty common fodder for us when people realize that our field touches on topics such as risk and decision analysis. "So, if I buy lottery tickets and I know that the chances of winning are supposedly really small, am I just throwing away my money or is there some way to boost my chances?" Needless to say, we are never short of advice (as this is the whole point of this book), and it mostly follows these lines, "You would most likely get a better return using other investment vehicles, such as savings account or bonds. On the other hand, lotteries can be really fun as long as winning is not part of your retirement planning. So if you want to have it as part of your entertainment budget, go ahead, knock yourself out." When really pressed, we may digress into more detailed discussion on expected value and whether anyone can justify playing the lottery, but by that point most of our audience will have moved on.

Let us assume that you bought 20 scratch-and-win lottery tickets. What would be the total return for all tickets if the price for one ticket is $1? In other words, if you spent $20, how much should you expect in return? In fact, over the past several years, we have been conducting an ongoing experiment on this exact subject. When we have our presentations on risk and decision analysis, we buy $20 worth of scratch-and-win lottery tickets, which we give out at random to attendees. During the presentation, we have the attendees check their tickets. The results have been very consistent. After spending $20 for tickets, the payout has usually ranged from $7 to $12: we have never won more than we spent on the tickets.

The theory behind this is very straightforward. Only a certain percentage from the ticket sales revenue goes toward prizes, normally around 50%. So the overall chance of winning a lottery is around 50%. The rest is used to pay costs for marketing and sales, but the vast majority of the owner's take is pure profit, which usually gets funneled into public goods or charities, so we do not feel so badly about the extended losing streaks that are common for those who play the lottery: "If it wasn't for the lottery, we would have to pay more taxes." Sort of like a bitter medicine with a tiny bit of honey. In this case, $0.50 is the *expected value* of playing one game. So why would people play under such measly payout conditions? Quite simply, there is a small chance to win a prize that is exponentially larger than the cost of the tickets. It is because of the potential for the large payout, we would also argue, that playing the lottery is a rational behavior. When discussing this with an acquaintance who participates in an office lottery pool, who also happens to be both a professional statistician and an avid gambler, he said, "Of course I know all about odds, but somebody is winning!" Therefore, in each particular game, you may win more or less than the expected value. Risk-takers hope that they will receive more than the expected value. Risk-averse people see the equation from the other side and believe that the chances are that they will receive less than the expected and therefore do not play.

> *Expected value is a probability-weighted average of all outcomes. The decision can be made by comparing the expected value of different scenarios.*

Expected value is not the prize you expect to win. If there is a million-dollar lottery, the expected value is not the prize. Rather, expected value is an indicator or a measure that will help you make better choices in uncertain situations. Expected value is calculated by multiplying each possible outcome by its probability of occurrence and then summing the results. Expected value can be calculated based on any parameters that are possible to measure, such as cost, price, duration, or number of units.

Take a look at Question 1 in our Judgment Test. When you multiply the probability of the payout for each one of Conrad White's alternative projects, you would get an expected value for the alternative. The alternative with the highest expected value (the city councilor position) would bring Conrad White the most money.

Situations when we can use simple expected value calculations arise all the time. When you buy a couch in a furniture store for $1,000, the salesman will probably offer you damage insurance for around $50. Without insurance, let's estimate that it would cost you about $200 to repair any damage. In addition, the chance that your couch will be damaged such that it will require a repair is 10%. In this scenario, the expected value of a repair is $200 x 10% = $20, which is significantly less than insurance cost. Therefore, unless you have five boys who like to bounce up and down on your couch with swords, forks and scissors, you should probably pass on the insurance.

Expected value will help you decide on a course of action in more complex cases. For example, lawyers use expected value when they make recommendations to their clients regarding possible legal actions. Would it be better to take a plea bargain and plead guilty to lesser charges or face the chance that you might lose at trial? Oil companies use expected value to calculate the volumes of oil and gas they can produce given uncertainties in petroleum reserves. Sales managers can use expected value to estimate sales figures. Governments are supposed to use expected value to estimate potential tax revenue. Since most governments are pathologically in debt, whether they understand the concept is open to question, or perhaps they just use unrealistic probabilities (100%) when performing expected value analysis on revenues.

For project managers, expected value is a simple and very effective analytical technique that can help us reduce the effect of many project illusions. It is a mostly simple mental exercise and is part of the project management process described in the PMBOK® Guide, Chapter 11 (Project Management Institute 2013). How much will the project cost given the chance of delay? Since there is always a chance that a supplier may not be able to deliver components on time, which supplier should you choose?

Let's return to our discussion on lotteries. If your idea of winning is getting more money out than you put in, then our recommended strategy is "Don't do it." However, if you find that you cannot help yourself, here we have another suggestion. Pick a number that appears to be non-random (e.g. 1, 2, 3, 4, 5, …). It will not increase your chances of winning, but if you win, you will be less likely to share the prize with someone else. Why? Most people think that these numbers are not random enough and don't select patterns. In reality, 1, 2, 3, 4, 5 is as random as any other combination of numbers.

How Project Managers Ignore Expected Value

The advantage of expected value is that you do not need to perform any complex calculations. You simply multiply probabilities on possible outcomes for different scenarios and then compare the results. Even though it is simple, people do not bother to do these calculations even though substantial sums may be at risk.

In 2005, an administrative law judge, Roy L. Pearson, filed a civil case in the District of Columbia. He claimed that a dry cleaning company had lost his trousers. Over a period of time, the owners of the dry cleaning business made three settlement offers of $3,000, $4,600, and $12,000 respectively, all of which were rejected by Pearson. Claiming the shop's "satisfaction guaranteed" sign misled customers, Pearson sought $1,500 for every day the dry cleaning operation was in business over a four-year period of time, or $54 million. Needless to say, the case generated a significant amount of attention and ridicule. *Fortune* magazine listed the case at No. 37 in its "101 Dumbest Moments in Business" of 2007 (*Fortune* 2007). Eventually, after years of working its way through the legal system, a federal court rejected Pearson's appeal (Alexander 2009). Pearson must be a real risk-taker. What was the chance that he would be successful in getting $54 million for a lost pair of pants? We imagine that he was probably angling for a lavish settlement rather than public humiliation. One can always make the case that Pearson did perform an expected value analysis; it is just that his assumptions must have been horribly skewed, so perhaps he is now working for the government providing tax revenue forecasts. In any event, Pearson's poor decision regarding the expected value of his legal actions managed to increase the misery of not only himself, but also the unfortunate owner of the dry cleaning business. As it turned out, the pants in question were never really lost; the dry cleaners had merely misplaced them temporarily.

While it may surprise some of our leaders, union leaders often have a good understanding of the underlying business situation facing their employers and use this knowledge to negotiate realistic compensation packages. On the other hand, there are also many examples where they ignore expected values and reality. In 2007, union members employed by the Greyhound bus company in Western Canada went on strike (Komarnicki 2007). One week into the strike, after it had caused millions of dollars in lost revenue and wages, the union accepted a new offer from the company. Notably, this offer was less than the original offer that had sent the union to the picket line. Union leaders probably were so overwhelmed by their membership's negative emotions towards management that they acted rashly without first performing an analysis that should have included an expected value for their final decision.

Intentionally or unintentionally overlooking expected value analysis is very common in project management. Large construction projects may have to go through an environmental assessment, which could be a long and very expensive process that would significantly delay the project and, therefore, increase project cost. A valid question may be to ask what value the assessment actually brings to the project. Does it actually protect the environment or would it be better to just save the money spent on the assessment and spend it on activities that actually protect the environment? It is possible to make a calculation based on the expected value principle; however, the validity of the bureaucratic procedures are rarely scrutinized.

Although in some industries, such as oil and gas or pharmaceuticals, expected value analysis is performed quite routinely, it is seldom seen in others, such as IT. IT project managers calculate the cost and duration of projects, but often forget that there is always a probability that something may not work according to plan. Failure to include the notion of probability to the analysis is one of the critical mistakes in project planning.

Incorrect Probability and Incorrect Expected Value

There is another issue with adoption of the expected value approach. How can we be sure that the estimated probabilities and outcomes are correct? For example, you have decided to purchase a new home and have two options (see Figure 10.1).

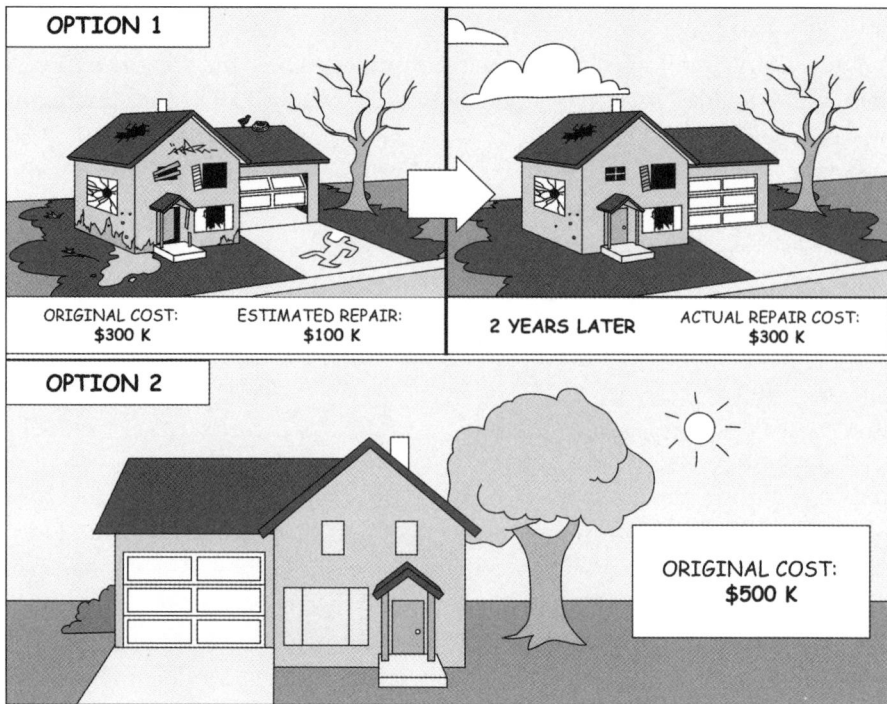

Figure 10.1   Who would buy a cheap, run-down home?
Source: Alex Alexeev.

a)   You can purchase a home for $300,000, but it will require an additional $100,000 for renovations.

b)   You can purchase a brand new home for $500,000.

If everything was straightforward, the first option would be the obvious choice, even taking into account the hassles of managing the renovations: you would save $100,000. But in reality, nothing is ever this straightforward. While the home sales price is determined, the cost of renovations is subject to multiple uncertainties. Remember confirmation bias (Chapter 2)? Because you would like to make the renovations at as low a cost as possible, you may dismiss evidence that costs could be significantly higher. The contractor has warned you that they have no idea what shape the house is in until they start to remove some of the flooring and walls to reveal the underlying wood frame. It could be in pristine condition, but there is a chance, given the age of the house, that there will be significant rot, outdated plumbing, or electrical systems that are not up to current building codes. If any of these conditions are present, it will drive up the cost of the renovations; and if more than one of these conditions is present – and this is likely given the age of the home – it will significantly drive up the cost. In the end, you determine that there is really only a 20% chance that the cost will be $100,000, and an 80% chance that the cost will be $325,000. Therefore, the expected cost of the renovation would be:

$$20\% \times \$200,000 + 80\% \times \$325,000 = \$300,000$$

After this analysis, option (b) (buy a new home) becomes much more attractive than option (a). This is why it is so important that probabilities are estimated as accurately as possible. If you underestimated the probability that the house would require more extensive renovations, not only would you be out of pocket by a lot more money, but you would have to live with the reality that you paid an extra $100,000 to live in a worn-out home, an issue that would probably become a popular topic of discussion with your spouse. So performing expected value analysis before making decisions not only saves projects, but can do wonders for your marriage as well.

Large projects have the same issue with assessing probabilities. The "Big Dig" was the unofficial name of the Central Artery/Tunnel Project (CA/T), a transportation megaproject in Boston, and is a good example of where the expected value analysis would have contributed to better, less costly decisions (Figure 10.2). The Big Dig had at the time the dubious record of being the most expensive highway project in the U.S. Originally in 1985, total project cost was estimated at $2.8 billion (in 1982 dollars); by 2006 total accumulated costs were over $14.6 billion ($8.08 billion in 1982 dollars) (Kwak 2008). Cost overruns were mostly attributed to politics, added scope, and problems with oversight. In particular, inflation and growth in scope added $2.7 billion, environmental compliance added $3.0 billion, and an accelerated schedule added $0.6 billion.

One issue that arose during the project was that the project management plan was based on an inadequate survey of the central artery. To save time and money, project planners took a risk and did not perform a detailed survey of this key feature of the project. With great hindsight, we can now say that, as in many cases, this attempt to save money led to spending more. The failure to perform a comprehensive survey had a direct cost to taxpayers of $26 million and perhaps much more due to indirect effects.

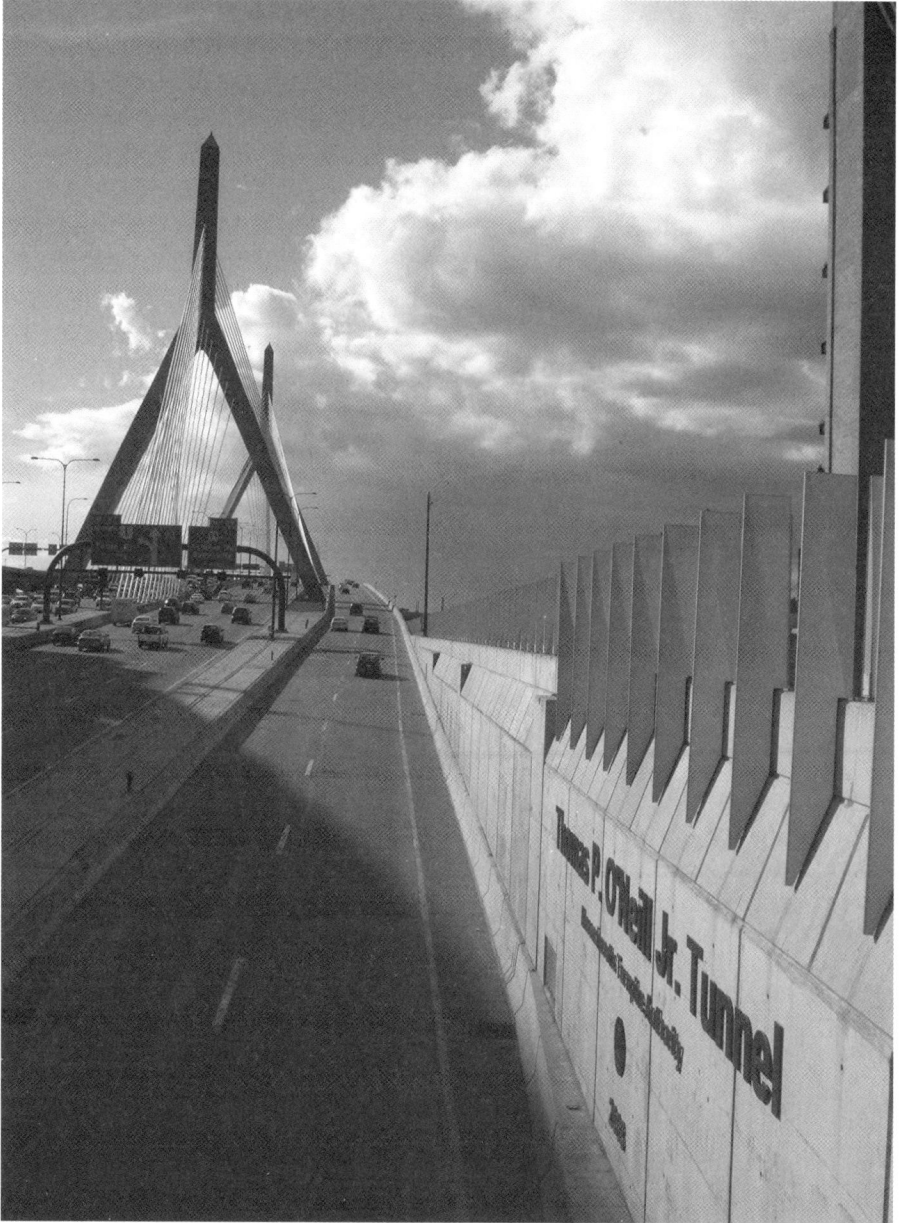

Figure 10.2   Traffic exiting the Big Dig tunnel onto the Zakim Bridge
Source: Arnold Reinhold, Wikipedia.

Another serious issue was related to the large number of water leaks in the tunnels. The contractors used a proven technology called "slurry wall panel" to create the tunnels, but in this particular case, the technique led to approximately 1,100 leaks that needed remediation.

Risks were not only technical in nature, but political as well. Local politicians caused an uproar when they discovered the water leakage in the tunnels. In reality, the extent of the leakage was insignificant and did not pose any threat to the integrity of the tunnels. Nevertheless, the project team was forced to bend to accommodate the concerns of the politicians and contractors were ordered to seal all of the leaks. In the end, it was the cumulative effect of all of these events that caused the huge cost overruns. Expected value analysis of different technological scenarios would potentially discover the level of exposure these risks represented and help the project team select a better plan for the project.

How to Choose a Scenario Based on Multiple Conflicting Objectives

So we have shown how you can calculate the expected cost, expected duration, and expected effort for different project scenarios. But how can we apply this same technique if decisions must be made using different objectives: cost vs. safety, finish time vs. quality, duration vs. technological advancement.

Here is how you can approach these types of problems. Let's assume that you are faced with a choice: hire a contractor or proceed with the project internally (Table 10.1).

Table 10.1   Making choices based on multiple criteria

	Hire a contractor	Proceed with project using internal resources
Duration	5 months	7 months
Cost	$180,000	$40,000
Probability of success	50%	60%
Expected value	$90,000 or 2.5 months	$24,000 or 3.6 months

So 1.1 months of project acceleration would cost you an extra $64,000. Does it make sense to do it? It depends on your project's or your company's particular situation. If you have significant budget and you have a firm deadline, you probably should hire a contractor. If you don't have extra money, but you may complete the project later, the second scenario will be appropriate. The problem happens when you don't have both time and money. In this case, you may need to perform analysis using *multi-criteria decision-making* techniques.

If you would like to perform this type of analysis, you should identify some objectives you would like to achieve. Here is a list of common objectives:

- minimize **cost**

- minimize project **duration**

- maximize **safety**

- **security**

- minimize **legal** problems

- maximize use of advanced **technology**

- minimize **public relations** problems

- maximize **quality**

- minimize impact to the **environment**.

There could be many other objectives; for example, you could ensure that you can operate in different geographical areas or jurisdictions, ensure high employee satisfaction, and others. The idea behind all multi-criteria decision-making techniques is that you assign weights and/or calculate priority for different objectives, and then measure your project performance against these objectives taking into an account these weights or priorities. For example, safety could be five times more important than cost. Or one month of work would be equivalent to $50,000: would you rather spend an extra $50,000 or delay the project for one month? After you assign weights, you may calculate a score for each project alternative. The score can be in any units: dollars, duration units, or just points, since it may be hard to assign dollar or duration values to such objectives as safety or security.

There are quite a few different multi-criteria decision-making techniques. For additional information, we cover this topic in more detail in our book *Project Decisions: The Art and Science* (Virine and Trumper 2007).

SMART TIPS

- Use expected value analysis to improve the quality of your decisions. It requires small calculations, which can be done without any specialized tools.
- Expected value analysis is part of the family of choice engineering techniques that does not require implementation of complex project management processes.
- Accurate assessment of probabilities is critical in performing meaningful expected value analysis.

11

Project Risks and Mental Errors

At the time of uncertainties and risks,
the most important thing is not to lose a head.

Marie Antoinette (allegedly)

In this chapter we will learn how to estimate the probability and impact of different events. We will also try to answer another question: what to do with the risks identified in Chapter 13 of this book. Risk assessment is not trivial as it is subject to multiple mental errors. Among them are zero-risk bias, loss aversion, ignoring base rate frequencies, gambler's fallacy, overestimating the probability of compound events, and others. People's response to risk and uncertainty varies due to the different risk attitudes of individuals and groups. Risk attitude measures how much risk an individual or group is willing to accept and is based on different factors, including emotions and biases.

Which Risk Is the Most Dangerous?

As you go about your life at home, at work and even on vacation, you are surrounded by a myriad of risks. When you step out of your door having managed to avoid a house fire, you could be hit by debris from a plane flying overhead or struck by a falling branch. According to official statistics, 600 Americans each year fall out of bed and die (Kluger 2006). When you wake up, you are at risk from heart attacks and poisoned toothpaste. When you go to work, you might collide with a lamp pole or die in a car accident. Finally, having successfully avoided all of these risks, you arrive at work and discover that there is now a risk that your project will be over budget by 5%. Compared with the risks with lethal consequences you have just avoided, the overbudget project should be your least concern. Nevertheless, for some reason, you are more preoccupied with project delays and far less so with traffic accidents. You might ask how we made this assumption. Well, you are reading this book, not *How to Survive Electrocution and Common Fatal Accidents* or *How to Avoid Falling out of Bed*. In fact, 411 people died from electrocutions in the U.S. in 2001, or

0.63 per million (Wrong Diagnosis 2008). At the same time, we are unable to find any official statistics on how many project managers died due to budget overruns.

Many of the difficulties in projects we cause for ourselves because we are not able to rationally assess risks. What project delay and cost will occur if management lays off the IT analyst? What is the chance that the software developer will attempt to use a new, untested software tool? In this chapter, we are going to learn how mental mistakes affect our assessment of the probabilities and impacts of risks.

Are You Afraid of Falling Asteroids?

Do you think asteroids represent a real danger? Should we do something to protect Earth against asteroids? Here are a few facts about asteroids:

1. The probability that a big asteroid would hit the Earth from now until its final destruction (an estimated 4 billion years from now) equals 1.

2. There are no confirmed human deaths due to asteroid impacts.

3. The chance of being killed by an asteroid on an annualized basis is somewhere between the chance of being killed by a shark attack and bee stings (Lynch 2008). This means that if you are concerned about being killed by a shark or a bee, you should be concerned about asteroids as well (Figure 11.1).

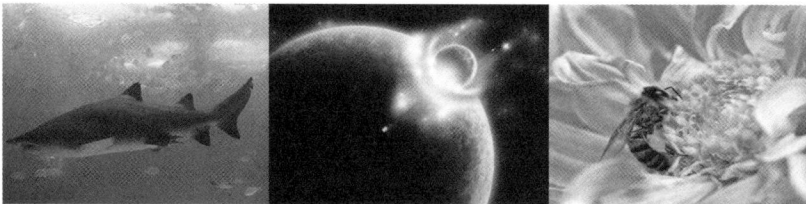

Figure 11.1   The chance of being killed by an asteroid is between the chance of being killed by a shark and by a bee sting

Source: iStockPhoto and Sajjad Fazel, Wikipedia.

What we are illustrating here is our analysis of this risk; we determined the probability for the risk and compared it with the probability of other risks. By doing this, we put the information regarding a potential asteroid impact into perspective. Based on this information, we can make an informed decision regarding how we should view this risk. It happens that the risk of asteroid impacts is a real one and real projects are under way to reduce these risks. Apparently reducing the probability of the risk by blowing it up with a nuclear blast (see the movie *Armageddon*) does not appear to be a good idea. More likely, in the event that a large asteroid's orbit takes it into close proximity to Earth, it may be possible to deflect it using either a nuclear blast or by hitting it with a heavy, fast-moving probe. So we are not completely doomed.

The problem with risk is that people often do not perform the necessary level of analysis and, even when they do, the results may not be very intuitive. To further complicate things, different people and organizations have different *risk attitudes* which affect their decisions.

What is Risk Attitude?

Built in 1985–89, the Sayano-Shushenskaya hydroelectric power station on Yenisei River in Siberia was the sixth largest hydroelectric power station in the world, with three times the power-generation capacity of the Hoover Dam (Figure 11.2). You may now be wondering why we are talking about it in the past tense. On August 17, 2009, the Sayano-Shushenskaya hydroelectric power station violently broke apart, flooding the turbine hall and engine room. The ceiling of the turbine hall collapsed, 9 of the 10 turbines were damaged or destroyed, and 75 people were killed (Demchenko et al. 2009). The entire plant output of 6400MW, a significant portion of the supply to the local grid, was lost, leading to widespread power failure in the local area and forcing all major users in the region, such as aluminum smelters, to switch to diesel generators.

How did it happen? As it turns out, turbine 2 had had a long history of problems prior to the 2009 accident. The turbine underwent a number of repairs, most recently from January to March 2009 in response to an elevated vibration emanating from it. By the beginning of July, the vibration exceeded specification and continued to increase with accelerated speed. On the night of August 16–17, the vibration level jumped substantially.

Figure 11.2   Sayano-Shushenskaya hydroelectric power station before the accident

Source: MVVAlt, Wikipedia.

By the following day, the vibration levels were extreme and were now registering with seismic instruments in the plant. During attempts to shut it down, the rotor inside the turbine was pushed up, which in turn created pressure pushing up on the turbine cover.

At 08:13 local time there was a loud bang from turbine 2. The turbine cover shot up and the 920-ton rotor shot out of its seat. Water spouted from the cavity of the turbine into the machinery hall. As a result, the turbine hall and rooms below were flooded. At the same time, an alarm was received at the power station's main control panel and the power output fell to zero, resulting in a local blackout. The steel gates to the water intake pipes of the turbines, weighing 150 tons each, were closed manually by opening the valves of the hydraulic jacks keeping them up. Seventy-four people were later found dead while one person is listed as missing.

Turbine 2 had major structural defects since its installation. Some of these defects were known well before the accident. A former power station director actually warned about the potential problem 10 years before the accident. Nevertheless, the automatic system which was designed to shut off water flow in case of high vibration was not engaged. Before the accident, when vibration increased dramatically, it was possible to perform an emergency shutdown of the turbine by shutting down the water flow. But apparently, in this case the people who were operating the station did not understand the potential risk impact of a turbine failure. In other words, the people who were trying to fix the problem before the accident and those who operated the troublesome turbine had a high risk tolerance: they were willing to accept a higher level of risk.

> *Risk attitude is the chosen response of an individual or group to risks and uncertainties.*

People always have an attitude towards risk. David Hillson and Ruth Murrey-Webster (2007) suggested a spectrum of risk attitudes (Figure 11.3 and Table 11.1). The vertical axis of Figure 11.3 represents uncertainty; the horizontal axis represents different individuals or groups.

Table 11.1   Risk attitudes

Risk Paranoid	a.k.a. Melvin Udall (Jack Nicholson) from the movie As Good as It Gets, a cranky, bigoted, obsessive-compulsive writer
Risk Averse	a.k.a. Felix Ungar (Jack Lemmon) from The Odd Couple, a neurotic, neat freak news writer who is thrown out by his wife
Risk Seeking	a.k.a. Marko Ramius (Sean Connery) from the movie The Hunt for Red October, a decisive Russian navy captain who hijacked a nuclear submarine
Risk Addicted	a.k.a. Indiana Jones (Harrison Ford), who miraculously survives extremely risky encounters with enemies, deadly beasts, and dangerous traps, but the number of these miracles exceeds any reasonable limits

We mentioned before that it is not just individuals, but also groups, such as companies, that possess a certain attitude towards risk (Hillson and Murrey-Webster 2008). For example, the street gangs from *West Side Story* were risk-seeking. Apparently, the same could be said for the banks and financial companies at the center of the 2008 subprime mortgage crisis.

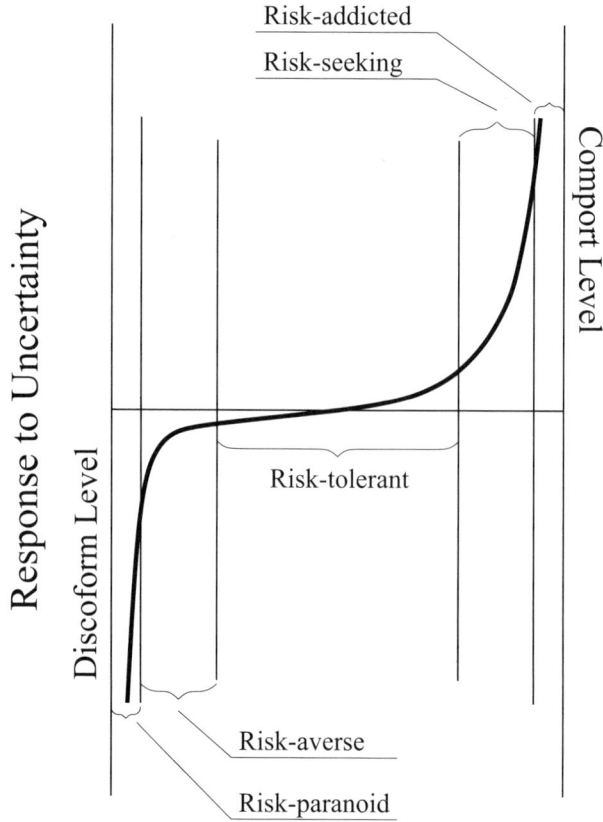

Figure 11.3   Spectrum of risk attitudes
Source: Original image is in Hillson and Murrey-Webster (2007: 63, Figure 5.2). The image has been modified.

Some organizations, especially large companies in traditional areas such as oil and gas and manufacturing, are risk averse. They significantly reduce activities during downturns in the economy even though it will potentially lead to losses over the next few years. Management of organizations comprises individuals who have their own risk attitudes. At the same time, the attitude of an organization will affect the risk attitudes of members of the organization. The question is: how does this risk attitude form and change over time, and why do different people and organizations have different risk attitudes?

Why People Have Different Attitudes towards Risk

Why, after failed terrorist plots to explode a commercial airplane, do authorities and ordinary people become very agitated? New security measures are put in place and people are transfixed to the news for days, surfing the Internet or TV channels for news regarding this newly emerging threat. We hear about an emergency landing due to unruly passengers, suspicious devices, and sometime because flight crews panicked by mistake. However, after a period of time we see that the heightened security measures are relaxed and the public becomes more complacent. Then this cycle repeats again and again. It leaves us with the impression that additional security measures are really just a type of "security theater" and have little to do with preventing terrorist attacks, but rather are designed to show the public that authorities are doing something by imposing extra hardship and inconvenience on travelers.

> *Dread factor: people tend to be less concerned about risks that are not catastrophic, but are controllable and are easily reduced.*

With some analysis, it is easy to see why this cycle will repeat itself endlessly, ad nauseam, into the foreseeable future. After an attempted attack, people's emotions, particularly fear, lead to a significant shift in risk attitude from risk tolerance to risk aversion and even to risk paranoia. In the Hillson/Murrey-Webster diagram, this would be seen as a shift to the left (see Figure 11.3). Interestingly, the more we fear something, the more anxious we get, and the more anxious we get, the less precisely we are able calculate the odds of an event actually happening. This is the so-called *dread factor* (Slovic 1987). The result is what psychologists call *probability neglect*. Since most people's fear will be reduced after some time, the risk attitude soon shifts back to its base state. From this we can see that emotions are one of the major factors which determine risk attitude.

> *Unknown factor: people are less concerned about risks that are observable, have immediate effects, and are known to science.*

Do you remember the e-coli outbreak in 2006 when hundreds of people became sick due to bacteria found in spinach (CDC 2006)? There was a huge reaction, producers lost millions of dollars as produce was destroyed and consumer demand sagged due to fears of infection. How do you feel about the next potential bacterial outbreak lurking in our food chain? Not so much, we gather. This is the *unknown factor*, which affects our perception of risks.

People are more concerned about something they have not experienced yet (McComas 2010). In project management the unknown factor plays a very significant role, since organizations and individuals may not have experience in the particular tasks or activities. Project managers may perceive that activities related to new tools, new software, a new supplier, or new team members are riskier.

Another factor which affects risk attitude is the heuristics and biases, which we discussed in Chapter 7. Here are a few examples. Terrorism leads to stronger reactions because, according to availability bias, it is vivid and it is easy to recall a recent incident. Because of this, people can empathize with the victims, walk in their shoes as they lived through the attack and therefore their risk attitude shifts towards risk aversion. In project management vivid project failures, especially if there are very significant monetary, job losses, or legal consequences, affect risk attitude.

The representativeness bias causes people to judge certain objects, people, or events based on a representative category. For example, a project manager might think that there is a heightened risk in dealing with a certain supplier due to a previous issue with a different supplier from the same industry or region, even though the current and previous suppliers are from different companies with completely different processes.

Optimism bias, which we discussed in Chapter 2, also plays a significant role in forming our risk attitude. Psychological research shows that people systematically believe that they are less affected by risks than others. In other words, they believe that negative events are more likely to happen to other people and positive events are more likely to happen to them. This is called *unrealistic optimism* (Weinstein 1989). Here are a few explanations of why we have this mental error:

1. People, due to the representativeness heuristic, incorrectly place themselves in the wrong category. For example, criminals consistently place themselves in the category of "criminal masterminds" who will never be caught. Similarly, project managers consider themselves in the category "project management experts" and believe that project failures are less likely to happen to them.

2.   People interpret risk information in a self-serving manner. For example, if they have not seen any signs of an issue developing, though other team members have reported it, they tend to believe that it is not going to happen. Remember Murphy's Law: if something bad might happen, it will. One of the variations of this law states: if everything appears to be going well, you are missing something.

3.   People employ the "ego-defensive" mechanism to justify risky behavior. People will say that they took adequate precautions, which happen to be ineffective or irrelevant. For example, project managers who engage in a risky project often say that they performed some risk mitigation to lessen the impact, but it turns out that it is not relevant to the particular activity or project.

4.   People believe they have more control over a situation than they really do. For example, drivers believe that they are less likely to have an accident than passengers. This is called the *illusion of control*.

Unrealistic optimism is responsible for shifting risk attitude on the Hillson/Murrey-Webster diagram to the right towards risk seeking or even risk addiction.

Risk attitude is different based on the magnitude of the problems. For example, if you are considering investing 10% of your company's revenue into a particular project, you may be willing to take some risk. What if the project required 90% of the company's revenue? The risk you would assume would most likely be much smaller. Taking smaller risks where large investments are required is a rational course of action, but you need to make these decisions consistently. The following is fictional, but it is useful to describe a very common phenomenon. A beautiful young lady decided to embark on a very complex and ambitious project: she arrives in New York with one goal in mind – to move up the social ladder and end up at the pinnacle of high society. Central to her plan is marriage to a rich and well-connected bachelor, preferably young and handsome, but these attributes are not absolutely required. To seduce her target, she decides to take a risk and spend her money on a very nice and extremely expensive dress. At the same time, she decides not to invest more on a good apartment in a socially attractive area, though she has the funds at the time (Figure 11.4).

Figure 11.4   Her dress and her apartment
Source: iStockPhoto.

How should we judge her strategy? She took one risky investment, but did not apply the same risk attitude to another investment related to the same project. It is irrational and may have had something more to do with her attraction to a beautiful dress than her end goal. Do you think she will succeed in seducing an investment banker? Probably, but not because of the expensive dress.

Paradoxes with Estimation of Probabilities

Take a look at Question 2 in our Judgment Test. In a room of just 23 people there is a 50-50 chance of two people having the same birthday; boost that number to 75 and the chance is 99.9% (BetterExplained 2010). It seems counterintuitive: you would think that to have a 50-50 chance of two people having the same birthday the number should be significantly more. Nevertheless, it is statistically correct and you can find the actual mathematical proof in the reference we provided. This paradox shows how easy it is for mental errors to affect our estimation of probabilities.

Here is one more phenomenon. Take a look at Question 8 on the Judgment Test. James Bond had so many life-threatening situations that a real person would have died a long time ago from accidents, drinking, or multiple sexually transmitted diseases. However, the question is, taking into account the probability of survival from all events in just one movie, what is the chance he survives to kiss the girl in the closing scenes (Figure 11.5)?

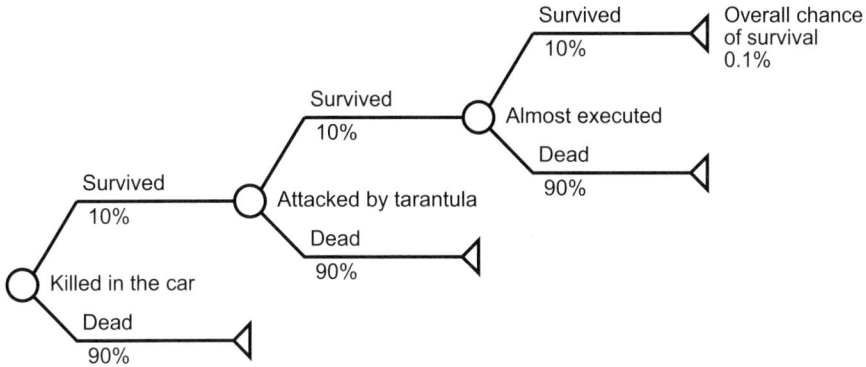

Figure 11.5   Probability of James Bond's survival

The overall chance of survival, which can be calculated by multiplying chance of survival in each attack, equals 0.01%. Most people will find this figure rather low and the phenomenon is called the *overestimation of probability of compound or conjunctive events*. It is very common in project management where managers overestimate the success rate of a project with multiple risks, which have a dependence upon each other.

Gambler's Fallacy and Statistical Independence

Take a look at Question 7 in our Judgment Test. Would our gambler's chance of winning increase after his many losses? Many people would say yes. In reality, statistically the chance of success remains the same. This is called the *gambler's fallacy* (Fallacy Files 2010). In many cases, the gambler's fallacy contributes to gambling addictions because people cannot stop playing as they believe that their "luck" will change and they will be able to recover their losses. Do you remember the movie *Vegas Vacation*? This is exactly what Clark Griswold (Chevy Chase) suffered from when he lost all his money.

A similar effect is called the *hot hand fallacy*. A gambler has had a streak of luck. Therefore, the gambler is either "hot" or "cold" depending on whether his luck is good or bad and the good or bad luck will continue at a probability greater than chance. Both fallacies are based on the same mistake; namely, a failure to understand statistical independence. Two events are statistically independent when the occurrence of one has no statistical effect upon the occurrence of the other.

Take a look at these sequences:

20, 22, 24, 26, 28

3, 7, 13, 20, 11, 31

In the first sequence the next number equals the previous number plus two. The second sequence is randomly drawn raffle ticket numbers. What should be the next number? In the first sequence it is 30. In the second sequence we cannot know. In project management, there are many events in which it is impossible to predict probabilities based on prior knowledge or if prior knowledge is insufficient. Nevertheless, people discern patterns where patterns do not exist or cannot be definitely identified.

For example, a team member may become sick. Despite the fact that it might be the flu season or the health of individuals may vary, particular events of sickness are hard to predict. Defects in devices or supplies can also be a statistically random event. Of course, some brands can have consistently higher quality than others, but within one brand there could be some defective units. So, it might just be your bad luck if you have a sticky accelerator pedal, even while the majority of the other accelerator pedals work perfectly fine.

Just remember not to be complacent and overly optimistic when developing your project plans and account for potential events even if they have yet to occur.

Loss Aversion in Project Management

Now, take a look at Question 3 in our Judgment Test regarding the movie *Pirates of the Caribbean 17*. Captain Jack Sparrow has a decision to make:

1.   100% chance to keep one gold nugget.

2.   50% chance to keep two gold nuggets.

We can look at the problem from another point of view. Sparrow has a choice:

3.   50% chance to keep both gold teeth.

4.   50% chance to lose both gold teeth.

According to the research (Kahneman and Tversky 1979), people would prefer a sure bet when they are dealing with gains and gamble when they are dealing with losses. In other words, people are willing to take more risks when they are going to lose something. This effect is called *loss aversion*. Psychologists noticed that losing $10,000 feels much stronger than gaining $10,000. Because of this effect the chart shown in Figure 11.3 is slightly asymmetrical. It means that discomfort level as a response to uncertainties often feels much stronger than the level of comfort.

In project management loss aversion manifests itself when people are more willing to take risk when they feel a threat and much more cautious when they are decided about exploiting opportunities. For example, if a project manager sees that the project is behind schedule, they are much more likely to request more resources. However, if an opportunity presents itself where they could complete the project much faster with higher quality, they are less likely to ask for more resources.

The loss aversion effect is not universal: several studies were not able to confirm the existence of loss aversion (Ert and Erev 2008). One of the explanations is that loss aversion does not exist when there are only small payoffs (Harinck et al. 2007).

Risks vs. Opportunities

Remember the movie *My Blue Heaven* starring Steve Martin and Rick Moranis? Vincent 'Vinnie' Antonelli (Steve Martin) is a former Mafia figure turned informant. While under witness protection in the suburbs, Vinnie becomes engaged in various criminal activities. The truck that is supposed to bring him supplies for his criminal businesses actually delivers empty water jars. "Somebody sees a problem, I see an opportunity," notes Vinnie and he decides to use the jugs to collect donations from his community towards the construction of a youth sport facility. In reality, his intent is to pocket the proceeds.

In spite of Vinnie's bumbling, he was absolutely right: in many cases, opportunities accompany threats. For example, a downturn in the economy can cause severe hardships, but it also presents an opportunity for many to successfully invest, start new businesses, or learn new technologies. Project delays are an opportunity to review issues, regroup, and improve management, not only for the current project but for other projects as well.

Most people know that risks and opportunities are related, but it seems to be counterintuitive. How can threats be converted to opportunities? Here is one explanation. In the same way that we are surrounded by a myriad of threats, we are surrounded by a myriad of opportunities. In most cases, we are so preoccupied with threats that we don't analyze opportunities. PMBOK® Guide has a risk management chapter which focuses primarily on the management of threats; in fact threats and risks are treated almost synonymously. There is no equivalent section on managing opportunities, although opportunities are mentioned. There are a number of risk analysis and risk management groups or societies, but they are almost all thought of as being preoccupied with threats. Perhaps the preoccupation of risk analysis on threats at the expense of opportunity analysis is related to loss aversion. However, when you start identifying and analyzing risks, realize that risks do not just represent threats, but are also opportunities staring you in the face.

Opportunities do not always coincide with threats. Sometimes the impact of a threat so quite severe that any opportunities cannot completely compensate for potential losses. However, it is important to remember that even in bad situations, there is room for opportunities.

SMART TIPS
- Make sure that you place yourself in the correct category when assessing your skills or expertise. If you mistakenly believe that you are an expert, it can cause unrealistic optimism bias and incorrect assessment of project risks.
- Try to determine your risk attitude: are you risk tolerant, risk seeking or risk averse? Use this knowledge to determine probability and impact of your project risks. Also, always know the risk attitude of your organization or of your team members.
- Opportunities often exist alongside threats. Try to identify opportunity for each risk.

PART IV
Choice Engineering

12

The Power of Adaptation

In Part III of this book, we discussed some simple ideas regarding how to improve your projects. In this part of the book we will learn how to set up project management processes which would lead to better decision-making in your organization or in your project team. In particular, we will focus on choice engineering: how to set up your environment so that it encourages people to make better choices. In this chapter, we will talk about one such choice engineering approach: adaptive management.

Processes Are Always Changing

For a number of years we consulted with a large high-tech company. The organization had a number of business units; each of them had a number of projects and programs. The process worked, but as always happens, there were some issues. The company hired a new CEO. Either because he had read something or somebody told him about it, the new CEO decided to create a project management office (PMO). It took a couple of years to understand how everything was supposed to work, train people, define roles and responsibilities, buy software, and perform some other activities to set up new the office. After two years, just when people were expecting to see some benefits from the new organization, the CEO left the company and a new CEO came on board. He had some new ideas and decided to dismantle the PMO and instead created project management centers of excellence. Work to set up the process started again: training, defining roles and responsibilities, software, etc. We recently heard that this CEO will be retiring shortly. What will happen next?

We often here criticisms of management for constantly changing strategies and priorities, but this reflects reality. The environment in which business operates is always changing, including product lines, objectives, organizational structure and management, and it can be very difficult to set up project management processes in this type of environment. One solution is to set up a system of structured and formalized project management processes. The PMBOK® Guide (Project Management Institute 2013) has 12 knowledge areas, which describe essentially 12 processes. In addition, there are many other processes not related to project management that must be followed. Just maintaining these processes can be the job for a whole team.

Another solution is to apply choice engineering whenever possible. As we have already learned from Chapter 3 of this book, choice engineering works by creating an environment in which people are steered, rather than policed, towards making better choices. It is much more flexible: since processes are lightweight and easier to set up and maintain. We mentioned such choice engineering principles as "full disclosure," templates and checklists, competition, and education. In this chapter we will give you another idea for choice engineering: adaptive management.

What Is Adaptive Management?

> *Adaptive management is a process of continually improving decisions by learning from the outcomes of previous decisions.*

Will polar bears become extinct because of climate change? Most likely not, as they, like all other living creatures, are capable of adaptation. Of course, if the climate shifts abruptly, as some have warned, no adaptations the polar bears make will help them find suitable habitats. But, if the climate changes are that extreme, the loss of the polar bear will be the least of our worries. Nevertheless, the ability to adapt is a distinctive feature of all life. Throughout our entire history, people have shown an incredible ability to adapt to almost any type of environment. Regardless of what you believe about man's role in affecting the global climate, the reality is that the climate is a dynamic system that has undergone significant changes over the course of Earth's existence, and if we are unable to moderate these changes (Harrabin 2007), we will have to adapt. As our environments change or shift, we have to defend against rising sea levels through better flood defenses, spending more on irrigation, growing drought-tolerant crop varieties, or if things get really cold, we may need to devise mechanisms to control the advance of glaciers.

In the 1970s, a group of ecologists that included C.S. Holling and Carl J. Walters (Walters 1986) researched how life forms adapt to their environment.

This research was trying to understand how fish stocks depend on many uncertain factors related to human activities. To meet this challenge, the scientists introduced the idea of adaptive management or adaptive resource management. Since then, adaptive management has become a key approach in the field of environmental engineering. Essentially, adaptive management is *"learning by doing and doing by learning."* It is a process for the continual improvement of decisions, management policies, and practices by learning from the outcomes of previous decisions. Examples of the implementation of adaptive management for large-scale natural resource management include projects in the Everglades and Grand Canyon National Park. The Department of Defense has been exploring adaptive management concepts for environmental cleanup at Navy facilities. The National Oceanic and Atmospheric Administration has utilized adaptive management for coastal habitat restoration activities (Linkov et al. 2006).

Adaptive management is a strategy that can be "adapted" for successful project management. It can be implemented as a structured and formalized process (Virine and Trumper 2007). However, we recommend introducing adaptive management as a set of guidelines or ideas as a choice engineering strategy. Here are a few adaptive management ideas:

1. Whenever possible, do not define a detailed project plan up front; instead, use an iterative project management approach.

2. Always identify multiple project alternatives or hypotheses; model these alternatives; and, if deemed beneficial, implement a few alternatives at the same time – alternatives which can be easily reversed are usually preferable.

3. Use analysis at each phase and iteration of the project, particularly qualitative or quantitative risk analysis.

4. Integrate original assumptions and new learning when planning the next project iterations.

Many engineers from different fields use a number of basic principles of adaptive management without actually understanding the work done by Holling and Walters. In 2001, a group of prominent software gurus met in the Snowbird resort in Utah to discuss effective software development processes. During the course of this meeting, they wrote *Manifesto for Agile*

Software Development (Manifesto 2006). This document offers a number of basic principles, which are similar to those of adaptive management:

- regular adaptation to changing circumstances, including changing requirements

- constant collaboration in project teams and with clients

- constant improving and refining processes

- iterative development processes.

The agile approach quickly became an effective project management methodology, not only for software development, but also for other industries. Adaptive project management as developed by ecologists is broader than agile processes. Analysis is key to adaptive management. In particular, adaptive management adds:

- multi-model analysis

- hypothesis testing

- actual performance measurement

- different types of risk and decision analysis.

How Adaptive Management Works

Let's assume that you are CFO of a large public corporation that is not meeting expectations. Your goal is to demonstrate good earnings to keep Wall Street analysts and investors happy. After sitting down and discussing the issue with your management team, you decide that you have four options:

1. Eliminate accounting and IT: they represent a cost on the balance sheet and do not produce any goods: lower expenses, higher profits. Who needs an MBA to come up with ideas like this and, best of all, your investors will love it.

2. Capitalize your operational expenses and then amortize them when

you do your taxes. It may be fraud, but this accounting procedure will significantly improve your balance sheet. Scott D. Sullivan, the former CFO of the now defunct WorldCom, tried it, investors loved it, but he ended up serving a four-year sentence. By capitalizing operational expenses, WorldCom hid $3.8 billion (Elstrom 2002).

3. Transfer your debt to subsidiaries: this will also improve your balance sheet, but you may find yourself in the same predicament as Andrew Fastow, previously employed at Enron, who was the resident expert in the tactic and later a convicted felon (Saporito 2002).

4. Accept the current loss of income and drop in share prices and concentrate on a corporate recovery program.

To evaluate all choices, make a decision, and execute your plan, you can apply ideas from adaptive project management processes (Figure 12.1).

These four choices are hypotheses, so before you go any further, you will need to test them. In order to test your hypotheses, you need to create a model for each one. It sounds very demanding, but in reality, it can be quite simple. For example, use expected value analysis as we discussed in Chapter 10 or create a project schedule for each hypothesis. Many project managers do not even use these very simple techniques to examine their options; sometimes they fail to even create a model at all.

If we look at the options, hypotheses 2 and 3 do not look very promising. While they would be simple to implement, their expected value includes a period of incarceration. Hypotheses 2 and 3 have another problem: they are irreversible. If you commit a crime, it is hard to reverse it.

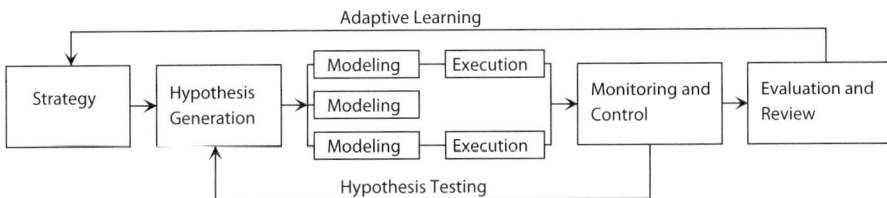

Figure 12.1   Adaptive management processes

One of the basic ideas of the adaptive management process is that your decisions should be reversible in case the decision happens to be wrong. But the other options, 1 and 4, could be implemented, which brings us to another important idea of adaptive management: multiple hypotheses can be executed at the same time.

So you decide to lay off IT and accounting because you are not sure what they do, but you know they cost a lot. As a result, they are always prime candidates for downsizing. At the same time, you are trying to improve the performance of your company (hypothesis 4). One month after your IT and accounting teams have been let go, you have been asked to report on the potential savings to the board of directors. Unfortunately for you, when you phone down to get someone to put together the report, no one picks up the phone. The accounting department is deserted. While you can deal with it – in a previous position it was your job to put together similar reports (you imagine it will be like riding a bike, once you learn, you never forget) – you are somewhat frustrated at the extra work. You start by asking your assistant to get you the financial data so you can start on the report. As it turns out, no one knows where the data is; that knowledge went out the door with your IT staff. You start to imagine options for your report: maybe you could deliver it as performance art, maybe a combination of puppets and a good light show would distract them from the fact that you have nothing to report. As luck would have it, you attended a seminar on adaptive management and understand that reversing previous decisions that have gone badly is considered good practice. While it may not look good at first – laying off people (most likely with severance packages) and then hiring them back – it is better than continuing on the current course. Now you are left with option 4 as your working hypothesis; it may not provide instant returns, but it will allow you to look at realistic ways of improving your company's performance. Even better, now that you have experienced this, you can record this as a lesson learned, which is the final step in the adaptive management process.

Barriers to the Acceptance of Adaptive Management

There is only one living species in the world that often actively resists adaptation – humans. In particular, project managers frequently do not realize that adaptive methods will bring better project results than traditional project management processes that include detailed project plans before starting execution. Many organizations embrace adaptive management methods and techniques. For example, many software development companies and teams actively use some principles of the agile approach. Nevertheless, traditional processes still dominate the field of project management. Why has there been such a slow adoption of adaptive management by project managers in particular industries? The answer lies in human psychology. There are a number of psychological biases that prevent people from accepting adaptive principles.

Tendency to Be Consistent

Recall the 2004 U.S. presidential election. President Bush's campaign rolled out a television ad that showed Senator John Kerry windsurfing and claimed his positions shifted whichever way the wind blows. In fact, Bush's campaign spent a lot of time and resources to label Senator Kerry as a "flip-flopper," portraying him as an inconsistent leader who bows to political pressure. To a certain extent Bush's campaign succeeded: people profess not to like inconsistent politicians, as it hints at unpredictability.

Politicians often accuse each other of being inconsistent, which in this case is meant to be seen as a character flaw: "Three years ago you supported the war, now you are against it. Will you admit to being wrong then, or are you wrong now?" In reality, we would argue that consistency in the face of changing circumstances or new information is the character flaw. For example, if a politician did not initially accept the role of humans in global warming, but changed his mind after reading new scientific evidence, most people would agree with this decision. The world is always changing, new or additional information is revealed and decision-makers must adapt to the new information. In fact, the best politicians, leaders, and managers are those who adapt to changing circumstances rather than sticking to outdated strategies or policies

People become uncomfortable if they are accused of being inconsistent. This is a common tactic used by both police interrogators and lawyers. They try to put people in a position in which they make inconsistent statements that causes the subject to be uncomfortable and provides a psychological advantage to the interrogators. Interrogations can last for hours; the person being interrogated will be extremely stressed and have trouble remembering what they said earlier. Once the interrogators spot an inconsistency, they can point this out, and in trying to explain these inconsistencies, some truths may be revealed. On the other hand, many innocent people have been convicted due to this process. If you ever find yourself in this situation, ask for a lawyer.

The tendency to appear consistent is very common in project management. When there is new information about a project and it is critical that decisions are made quickly to deal with the developing situation, the tendency to consistency is often an obstacle to selecting the best options. If a device does not work, sometimes it may not make sense to fix it; a better solution may be to build a new one. Project managers have to be willing to admit to errors and adapt to new circumstances.

In addition, even if individual project managers are capable of reversing decisions, the corporate culture may not support it. Senior management often frowns upon managers who stray from project plans. That is why if our previous example actually took place, we have serious reservations whether the CFO would re-hire accounting and IT even if there is strong evidence to support it.

Why do people tend to be consistent when adaptation is necessary? In fact, the tendency to be consistent is a manifestation of the sunk cost trap, which we discussed in Chapter 6. People are trying to protect previous choices even though the situation has changed.

Status Quo Bias

Let's assume that for 25 years you served as the president of the African Republic of Urbumbia. You were re-elected four times and now it is time for you to be re-elected again. The problem is, this time around people are unhappy with your ruling and polls show that you, for the first time, are facing a very serious threat from the opposition. Of course you can crack down on the opposition, throw them in jail on trumped up charges, or postpone the election for the next 10 years due to vague threats to national security. However, beginning your campaign of deception and human rights abuse, you might want to try something much simpler with a similar chance of succeeding. Call a press conference and tell the people, "Look, I know that you have suffered for the past several years and living standards have gone down, but at least you survived. But how is the opposition going to make your lives better? No one knows; they have no experience and you will probably suffer more. At least with me, you know what you are getting." You may be damning yourself with weak praise, but it will appeal to people's status quo bias.

In many situations, including projects, people resist change unless there is a really compelling reason to do it, most often because we believe that changes will make things worse (Samuelson and Zeckhauser 1988). For most people, despite how bad the current situation may be, knowing what to expect is a more comfortable choice than choosing the unknown. In addition, changes may cost a lot and without any guarantees of results. Psychologists explain status quo bias using the concept of loss aversion, which we discussed in Chapter 11 (Kahneman et al. 1991).

In project management, people often resist any changes in processes and polices and this makes it difficult to adopt effective adaptive management processes. Let's assume you are a project engineer at a car manufacturing plant and approach your manager with an idea to improve a technological process. Your project manager may tell you "no" based on a number of considerations: high cost, risk of failure which may cause a chain reaction across the whole manufacturing process, additional training requirements, and so on. In fact, before answering "no" he had probably already made up his mind without attempting any analysis. The real reason for his "no" answer would be his psychological resistance to the change. Status quo bias explains why ineffective project management procedures often are not changed and why outdated technology is not replaced.

SMART TIPS
- Whenever possible, try not to define a detailed project plan up front; use an iterative project management approach.
- Always identify multiple project hypotheses; model these hypotheses; and if deemed beneficial, implement a few of these models at the same time; hypotheses which can be easily reversed are usually preferable.
- Use analysis at each phase and iteration of the project, particularly qualitative or quantitative risk analysis.

13

What to Do About Risks

In Chapter 11, you learned about the various psychological phenomena that can affect your perceptions of risk. In this chapter we are going to learn how to deal with risk. You may be familiar with the PMBOK® Guide, which describes a formalized approach to risk management. We are going to use a slightly different approach and focus on how choice engineering can be used for managing project risk. We will discuss a few simple techniques that you can use that will improve your ability to handle risk during the course of your projects.

Make It Simple

A couple of years ago we participated in a risk management conference for the aerospace industry. One of the presentations was titled "Risk Management for Human Space Exploration" and drew an especially large crowd. There were a couple of hundred engineers, researchers and students who gathered to learn about how to manage space exploration risk from a representative of one of the largest aerospace organizations in the world. However, topics did not cover risks associated with hostile aliens, deadly space debris, or black holes; instead attendees were presented with descriptions of the multiple regulations, procedures, directives, rules, and other documents which regulate risk management in these organizations. It was mind-boggling to see how many documents are created by one particular organization for what is really quite a narrow subject. It probably took at least a dozen man years to write them. Merely showing an extremely compressed version of these documents caused mass lethargy in the audience. In fact, the presenter himself almost seemed to take on the persona of a hypnotist, droning on and on, seemingly intent on putting the crowd in a trance. It may well have happened, for after the presentation ended and the lights snapped on, it was as if the hypnotist had snapped his fingers to bring his subject out of hypnosis. People wandered out of the presentation with a slightly mystified look, unable to recall many details of the past hour. This is really not the effect you are going for when you discuss risk processes.

In reality, risk management processes should be relatively simple, especially when you are trying to establish them. To help simplify the processes, choice engineering should be the main foundation of your risk management processes. Along these lines, you should first look to establish a few unobtrusive procedures which will steer people towards using better judgment regarding risk.

Consider these three issues:

1.   What events might occur during your project and what would be the impact of these?

2.   What is the probability that they will occur?

3.   What can we do either to minimize or take advantage of these events?

Many problems occur in projects because, for one reason or another, people fail to ask these questions. When something happens during a project and causes a major problem and you ask why it happened, most project managers, if they were honest, would answer, "We just did not think about it."

Risk management guidelines, procedures, and regulations often hide the most important thing about risk management: it is a *thinking exercise*. So start with these three questions. Later on, when you are more confident, you can begin asking a few more questions, such as what triggered or caused this risk, what is the cost of the risk if it occurs, and so on. The process constitutes *qualitative risk analysis*. If you wanted to perform a more detailed statistical risk analysis based on your project schedule, we refer to this as *quantitative risk analysis*. If you are interested in finding out more about this, it is covered in detail our book *Project Decisions: The Art and Science* (Virine and Trumper 2007).

To answer these questions, you should create a list of the risks with their probabilities (answer to Question 1) and their impacts (answer to Question 2). For example, before sending James Bond out to stop an evil mastermind from sabotaging the world's economy, we suspect that his managers would ask him to complete a quick risk list that they had put together as part of their risk engineering process (Table 13.1).

Table 13.1   Risk list of James Bond's project

	Risk	Probability	Impact
1	Drive on mountain road without brakes	50%	Minor project delay
2	Jump from top of skyscraper without parachute	40%	Minor project delay
3	Meet with beautiful, yet dangerous, woman	99%	Major project delay

Strategies for Dealing with Risks

Let's imagine the following situation. The American public tires of having lawyers, actors, and professional sport team managers as the President; instead, because a government is a set of complex projects, they elect a professional project manager to run the country. Moreover, due to your demonstrated prowess in delivering successful projects, you are elected Project Manager in Chief. In your first major international crisis, you are informed by your National Security Advisor that the Democratic Empire of Unlawful Lands (DEUL) has plans to launch a new computer virus that will destroy all text documents on infected networks. What should you do?

Remember that you need to ask your National Security Advisor three questions:

1.   What might happen during the course of your project and what would be the impact? If the virus is launched successfully onto a national computer network, it will destroy all of the text documents on the infected network.

2.   What is the probability that it might happen? Your National Security Advisor estimates that there is a 5% chance that it will be successful. To be more exact, it is better to use an actual percentage for probability rather than a verbal description. Why? If the National Security Advisor says that chance is minimal, you might think that it is 1%, and he may actually be implying that it is 10%. That represents a large difference in perception of the risk. State estimated probability as accurately as possible to avoid this type of confusion.

3. What can you do about it? This can be quite a difficult question
    to answer. As Project Manager in Chief, you have to decide what
    would be the best *risk management strategy* given all the possible
    outcomes of your decisions. Your National Security Advisor may
    give you a few options:

    a) Do nothing. In each set of choices these is always the
        option to do nothing. Perhaps it would not be such a bad
        thing if all the text documents were destroyed. It would
        certainly reduce red tape and bureaucracy. Unfortunately,
        the problem with bureaucracies is not the documents
        themselves, but rather the people who manage them. This
        "do nothing" option is called a *risk acceptance* strategy in
        risk management.

    b) Send agents to assassinate DEUL's president. This strategy
        will probably not eliminate the threat, as the president of
        DEUL is not actually the individual who would release the
        virus, but in theory, it may deter people from releasing the
        virus. This is called a *risk mitigation* strategy.

    c) Develop an antivirus program. This would also be a risk
        mitigation strategy, as the antivirus is not a 100% certainty
        and it may take some time to develop it. Essentially the risk
        has not been eliminated; just its probability and impact are
        reduced.

    d) Let the Canadian Prime Minister deal with it. This is called
        a *risk transfer*. Though it is unclear whether the Canadian
        Prime Minister would take on this risk unless you
        provided something in return; perhaps eliminating duties
        on softwood lumber might persuade him, but that would
        entail political costs. It is the same any time you transfer
        risk; there will be a cost as the party it is transferred to will
        expect some type of payment in return, for example if you
        purchase insurance against the risk.

    e) Decide to discontinue the use of computers and computer
        networks in the government – back to paper and abacus.
        This strategy is called *risk avoidance*. By eliminating the use
        of electronic documents, we manage to avoid the risk.

The only way that you as the President could select the best risk-handling strategy is to perform a more detailed analysis. We will give you an idea about how the President should select an alternative later, but before that, we will discuss how to compare different risks.

How to Build a Rocket, or Risk Ranking

What if rocket science was not actually rocket science? If you are not an aerospace engineer or otherwise employed by the industry, here is a simple explanation of how to build a rocket. Basically speaking, rocket design is a fairly straightforward process. At a high level, it requires only engines, fuel tanks, and a pay load. To ensure reliability, you can add many redundant systems, sensors, and enforce it to ensure it can withstand even the most extreme launch forces. Your rocket would never explode, but it would never fly: it would be too heavy. To decide which systems or components will have the most effect on improving reliability or safety and should be included in the design, engineers must analyze and rank multiple risks. The simple way to do it would be to multiply probabilities on impact. Risks with higher ranks should be mitigated or avoided first. In the case of James Bond's project (Table 13.1), the most important risk would be "Meet with beautiful, yet dangerous, woman" and the risk "Drive on mountain road without brakes" would be ranked second.

This type of process is used by engineers at the SpaceX Corporation. SpaceX is an American space transport company that builds the Falcon 1 and Falcon 9 rockets and the Dragon series of spacecraft that will be orbited by the Falcon 9 launchers (Figure 13.1). NASA is planning to use SpaceX rockets for resupplying the International Space Station after the Space Shuttle retires in 2010. During the planning of one of the early launches of the Falcon rocket, SpaceX engineers decided to mitigate their 10 most critical risks. For all remaining risks, they just chose to accept them as the most effective strategy. Almost predictably using hindsight, the launch failed because the 11th ranked risk occurred (Insprucker 2008).

But were the engineers incorrect in their ranking, or should they have chosen to include the 11th risk as part of their mitigation plans? We will review a potential solution later in this chapter.

Figure 13.1   Computer simulation of SpaceX's Falcon 9 and Dragon spacecraft lifting off from Cape Canaveral, FL

Source: NASA.

Should We Protect Commercial Airplanes Against Surface-to-Air Missile Attacks by Terrorists?

Do you protect yourself against dog bites? You could wear special Kevlar pants that would be difficult to bite through; you might instead opt to carry a T-bone steak with you that you could use to distract menacing dogs while you climb up the nearest tree. Or do you really put much credence to this at all? Sure, you might get bitten, but unless you are a mailman, we doubt that you are taking all necessary precautions. Why? Because if you have done a risk assessment, you would probably come to the same conclusion as pretty well everyone else around you: the chance that you will be bitten by a dog is very slight. In fact, this is an illusion. The official survey determined there were 4.7 million dog bite victims annually in the U.S. A more recent study showed that 1,000 Americans per day are treated in emergency rooms as a result of dog bites. In 2007 there were 33 fatal dog attacks in the U.S. and losses due to dog attacks exceeds $1 billion per year, with over $300 million paid by homeowners insurance (Dog Bite Law 2010). When you decide how to deal with potential dog attack, you intuitively determined the probability and, to a lesser extent, the impact of the risk. Since the probability and impact did not seem very significant, you decided not to take any precautions other than avoiding the attention of mean-looking dogs.

Here is another example. A few years ago, the government asked experts in decision analysis to conduct research on whether we should install special defensive equipment on commercial aircraft to protect against surface-to-air missile attacks by terrorists. One of the motivations behind this research was a failed attempt by terrorists in Kenya to shoot down an Israeli commercial airplane in December 2002 using shoulder-mounted missiles similar to the relatively compact Stinger missiles used in the James Bond movie *License to Kill* (Figure 13.2).

Here is a brief description of the problem the experts were asked to address. There is a chance that terrorists will try to use such missiles to shoot down planes. The anti-missile technology that they were considering is available for military planes, but it is very expensive. Can they, the government, justify the cost of installing this equipment on each commercial plane operated in the U.S. given the potential risk? The researchers first analyzed the chance that terrorists would be able to mount such an attack, and then the chance that one of these attacks would actually bring down a plane (von Winterfeldt 2008).

Figure 13.2   FIM-92 Stinger missile launcher
Source: U.S. Air Force.

Once they had determined this, they calculated the cost in monetary terms if the plane was lost. Finally, they calculated the cost of installing and operating the missile defense equipment on every plane. As it happens, it would be very expensive – millions of dollars per plane. The researchers concluded that unless the cost of the equipment was drastically reduced, it would not make any economic sense to install the devices. The results of the study were presented to policymakers and they agreed not to require the installation of these devices. The current risk management strategy is to accept this risk, at least for now.

You question whether a straightforward economic cost/benefit analysis is the right way to go about making this decision. What about the cost in human life and suffering, the grief of the loved ones? How can you measure that? Well, you can't, but you have to be able to use some measure to assess and make decisions regarding risk in a meaningful way. Analysis of the *potential loss* is a valid approach that will help you to decide on a course of action. The concept is very simple:

1.   Calculate the potential loss, which is the cost you will have to pay if the risk occurs. For example, as President you are told the potential loss due to the DEUL virus is approximately $100 billion.

2.   Calculate the cost of mitigation efforts. If you decided to develop an antivirus program, it is estimated to cost $10,000,000.

3.   Calculate total cost associated with risk: potential loss multiplied by probability of risk plus cost of mitigation efforts. In our example it would be $100 billion (potential loss of the virus attack) x 10% (probability) + $100,000 (antivirus development) = $10,000,100,000.

Zero-risk Bias

A friend of ours was very concerned about the risk of medical mistakes. Reading and hearing examples and statistics about medical mistakes had caused him to become quite anxious, so he decided to eliminate this risk by refusing to see a doctor regardless of his symptoms. No doctors – no potential mistakes – very straightforward solution. The problem was that he significantly increased his chances of another risk: the risk that if he got ill and it would go untreated.

A lot of people believe that the best strategy is to completely eliminate risk. However, completing eliminating risk can be extremely expensive and can cause other risks. In most cases, a better course of action is to reduce the probability and impact of risks in the most cost-effective manner. In our example with the threat of a computer virus, one option for the President is to completely eliminate the risk by ordering the government to discontinue the use of computers and computer networks (option e). While this would eliminate the risk, it would be very expensive and could trigger many other risks.

Zero-risk bias is common when people make decisions about health, safety, and environment. This bias often manifests itself in managing hazardous waste, using nuclear energy, and rules and regulations regarding public safety. If you want to completely eliminate an accident on an assembly line, you have two choices:

1. Replace all workers with robots, including those workers who maintain and repair the robots.

2. Shut down the assembly line.

A more realistic solution for the assembly line would be to use some robots in addition to additional safety measures to reduce the chance of accidents.

Risk Engineering

Bridges across rivers are designed to withstand large floods. But what if there is a massive, once in 100 years, flood? Floods like this will probably destroy most bridges, but it is not a design flaw. In fact, it is part of the construction code. Can a bridge be built to withstand these types of events? Of course it can, but it would be cost-prohibitive. Instead of having many conveniently located river crossings with fast-flowing traffic, you would have only a few and traffic would slow to a crawl. Since the chance that an extreme event is relatively small, it is cheaper to rebuild a bridge if it is destroyed rather than over-engineer it in the first place. Bridge engineers must select the right balance between different risk mitigation strategies to make this bridge cost-effective.

Risk engineering is a continuous process of balancing risk response strategies for different risks in the project or program.

Risk engineering involves accepting, mitigating, avoiding, and transferring certain risks in such a way that the final project is cost-effective and less risky at the same time. This requires that you analyze different combinations of risk management strategies on a full set of project risks.

When considering risk engineering, it is most important that it is performed continuously over the course of a project. During the project lifecycle, the risk management strategy may change based on new information. This balance between various risk-handling strategies will change as well. If as a result of the unsuccessful SpaceX rocket launch the 11th ranked risk is now considered critical for future launches, it must be avoided. However, since all risks associated with this rocket cannot be avoided, the strategy for another risk may have to be shifted from avoidance to mitigation. In the example we provided regarding the surface-to-air missile protection for commercial airplanes, the cost of such systems may go down. In this case, it becomes a viable response to switch the risk management strategy from acceptance to mitigation.

When Quantitative Risk Analysis is Necessary

John Brokennose is two things: a professional criminal and a poor project manager. He is currently serving time in a state penitentiary for a failed bank heist. He lent some of his tools to his son for his son's school science project and, as a result, did not have them with him when he tried to open the bank vault. Now he sits in his cell planning his next project, escaping from the prison. He has already created a preliminary plan (Figure 13.3). Here are his planned activities:

1.   Cut through bars on windows: estimate 30 minutes, but there is a 50% chance that his nail file will not be very efficient, which could add an additional 10 minutes.

2.   Jump from the window and carefully walk towards outside fence, avoiding discovery by guards. He estimates that it will take around 15 minutes. However, there is a 30% chance that the guard dogs might be alerted and start barking. Additional evasive maneuvers will cause a delay of 10 minutes.

3.   Climb the fence. John has noticed that the guard, T.I. Sherlokholmes, who will be on watch duty in the tower, spends 75% of his time talking on his cell phone to one of his three girlfriends and doesn't pay any attention to the fence during this time. John has to wait on average 5 minutes until one of the girlfriends calls. However, there is also a 10% chance that the guard will unexpectedly get a call from a new girlfriend, which will reduce his wait time by 5 minutes.

4.   Jump into his associate Jack Wideneck's car. Jack will be waiting for John outside of the fence.

The plan is simple. But there is one additional complication. Jack Wideneck cannot stop his car by the fence for long and John cannot wait for the car. The car must be underneath where John is waiting within a 10-minute window. The question is: when should John start to cut the bars to make sure that he lands in the car with 95% probability?

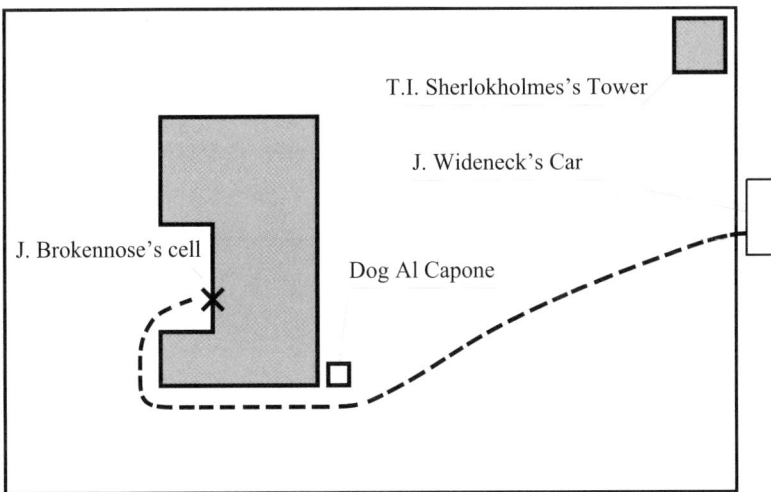

Figure 13.3   Prison escape plan

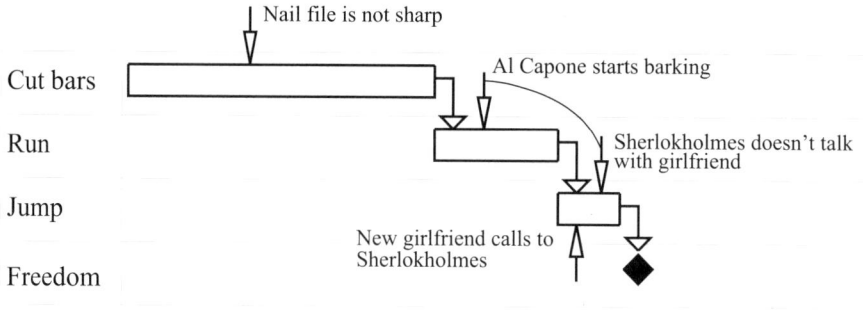

Figure 13.4   Prison escape schedule

This is an example of a situation when the question cannot be answered without quantitative analysis. John Brokennose must perform this analysis before starting his escape plan. To start with, he has to create a schedule (Figure 13.4) in the form of a Gantt chart. Then he draws risks associated with each task as arrows on the Gantt chart. The project has three threats and one opportunity (if a new girlfriend decides to call Sherlokholmes). Gantt charts with arrows representing risks are called *event chain diagrams*. Threat arrows point down, opportunity arrows point up – quite simple and intuitive. If threats or opportunities are related to each other, they are connected by a line. For example, if a guard dog starts barking, Sherlokholmes may stop his conversation with a girlfriend. The size of an arrow represents the probability of the risk. Event chain diagrams can significantly simplify risk analysis.

Now John Brokennose should use a software program to perform the analysis. He enters the project schedule and all risks, assigns risks to activities, defines their probabilities and impacts, and performs a calculation. For purposes of brevity, we will skip the mathematical details of how the calculation is performed.

The result of analysis shows that Jack Wideneck must wait in the car for John Brokennose for 22 minutes to ensure that there is a 95% chance that John Brokennose will not be discovered, which is significantly higher than John originally estimated. According to the analysis, the chance of a successful prison escape is only about 70%. John Brokennose is very risk averse and has to abandon the escape plan.

If John Brokennose wants to increase his chances of escaping from prison, he will have to perform some risk engineering. His prison escape plans includes three risks:

1. Nail file doesn't cut quickly enough. Originally, the chance that this risk would occur was 50% and the impact was a 10-minute delay. John believes he can avoid this risk by using a good hacksaw.

2. The guard dog starts barking. John Brokennose cannot do anything about this and must accept this risk.

3. Sherlokholmes does not speak with one of his girlfriends. Originally, there was a 25% probability that it would cause a delay of 5 minutes. What if John Brokennose finds an additional girlfriend for Sherlokholmes? This would reduce the probability to 15%.

Now we can perform this analysis again. The results show that Jack must park near the fence for 15 minutes to ensure that there is a 95% chance that John will cross the fence while the car is there and not be discovered. Better, but still not good enough; plus John needs to find a hack saw and a new girlfriend for Sherlokholmes. Perhaps John could try a different scenario to deal with the risks. He could slip some drugs into the dogs' food, which would mitigate the barking risk, and then he might have extra time and not need a hack saw. As part of risk engineering, we recommend an analysis that uses different risk management plans for each risk be performed multiple times to determine the best course of action.

Unfortunately most criminals do not perform risk analysis before engaging in criminal activities. If they did, they probably would not involve themselves in criminal activities in the first place. Project managers often follow the same path and do not perform risk analysis, in spite of the fact that they have all the tools at their disposal to ensure that they don't expose their projects to unnecessary risk.

SMART TIPS

Choice engineering for managing risk may include establishing a few very simple procedures:

- creating a list of risks
- determining probability, impact, and score for each risk
- ranking risks based on risk scores (probability x impact)
- choosing a risk-handling strategy.

These steps constitute simple qualitative risk analysis. In some cases, quantitative risk analysis is necessary.

14

Choice Engineering for Organizations

"Don't be evil"

Lord Voldemort

In Part I of this book you learned about choice engineering. In this chapter you will learn how choice engineering can be used to improve corporate culture and, as a result, improve the bottom line of your company. In some large companies, issues related to the corporate culture lead to disengaged employees and subsequent loss of productivity. You can learn a few choice engineering tricks that will create a positive working environment for your team members, your boss, and yourself.

Are You Borg?

Our favorite creatures in *Star Trek* are Borg. Just to remind you, the Borg are cybernetic life-forms thousands of years old who are part organic, part artificial life (*Star Trek* 2010). In the fictional universe of *Star Trek*, the Borg inhabit a vast region of space, possessing millions of space vessels, having conquered and assimilated thousands of civilizations. They operate solely toward fulfilling one purpose: to add the biological and technological distinctiveness of other species to their own in pursuit of perfection. How do they do it? They implant synthetic components, or nanoprobes, into each individual and, as a result, assimilate the individual into the *collective*. Also referred to as the "hive mind" or "collective consciousness," this is the term used to describe the group consciousness of the Borg civilization. Each Borg individual, or drone, is linked to the collective by a sophisticated subspace network that ensures each member is given constant supervision and guidance. The hive-mind drones do not register as individual life-signs when scanned, only as a mass reading. The Borg are also able to adapt quickly to any perceived threats. So entrenched has the idea of the Borg become in popular culture that it is common to refer to large organizations or bureaucracies (see the IRS) against which "resistance is futile" as the Borg.

Working in a company, we may get the sense that there is something irrational about the corporate culture or system, but due to social or professional pressures, we tend to push aside any unease we may feel and instead try to make the best of what could be a bad system. Moreover, if we hang on long enough, in spite of our initial misgivings, we may find ourselves actively supporting the system as we make our journey up the corporate ladder on our way to senior management. Why? We become the Borg (Figure 14.1).

> *Corporate culture which exists in many organizations leads to disengagement of employees and significantly affects the company's bottom line. It is one of the significant obstacles towards improving the company's productivity.*

Figure 14.1   Did you become a Borg?
Source: Alex Alexeev.

When we join an organization, it is as though we have been assimilated into a collective and we start to think as a collective. After a short while, this groupthink limits our creativity and we stop thinking outside of the box. This can lead to acquiescence and an expectation that somebody will make decisions for us; we start to ignore or not even notice problems with the organization; and, we begin to treat our subordinates in the same manner we are treated by our managers: as small parts of a complex mechanism designed to perform a very limited function.

But the main problem is that after we become assimilated into the Borg, we start to believe that system is normal. "Hive mind" prevents us from realizing that modern corporate culture often does not help to improve a company's performance and often hinders it. At the same time, resistance against the system is futile; we can develop learned helplessness. No matter what we do individually, it does not make a difference, so we become helpless.

Don't Be Evil!

This is the corporate motto of Google (Google 2010). In practical terms it means that Google should be measured against the highest possible standards of ethical business conduct in all aspects of the business: hire great people, who then build great products, which in turn attract loyal users. One of the most important components of this is a thriving corporate culture inside Google. For a number of years, Google has sat at the top of most lists as one of the best companies to work for (*Fortune* 2010). In addition to great compensation and many perks, such as 401(k) matching and stock-option exchange programs, Google engineers get to devote 20% of their time to projects of their choosing. This is central to Google's plan to create a productive environment that actively engages employees in their work and encourages creativity which should lead to better products and services for their customers and improve the company's bottom line. Does this concept remind you of something? We hope so. Google has adopted *choice engineering* as a key aspect of maximizing the company productivity, even though they do not refer to their policies in this way. Effective organizations avoid mandating certain choices as this creates a bureaucracy of rules, procedures, and regulations that by its very nature is counterproductive. Successful companies steer their employees towards making better choices using minimal policing and effective policies that stimulate employee creativity and engagement.

Disclosure Therapy

In Chapter 3, we discussed full disclosure as one of the key choice engineering principles. If you are an investor, you are probably familiar with the term full disclosure. In the investment world, full disclosure provides investors with all of the information regarding a company or other investment so that he or she can make an informed decision on whether to invest or not. It is an example of choice engineering: you provide them with information that would help them make choices that would increase productivity rather than simply urging them to be more productive. Disclosure therapy is not simply disclosing the financial state of the company; it also involves effectively communicating the who, what, when, where, and why of the corporate strategy. Most companies are reluctant to release some information to employees, such as plans for new product development because of a fear that their competitive information will be leaked. We understand the concerns of management in regards to the security of this type of information; however, the advantages of disclosing information to their teams should outweigh the risks of leaking this information to competitors. Of course, certain data (personal information, etc.) must be kept confidential, but data that will provide project teams with a clearer understanding of business opportunities or objectives should be disclosed.

What to Do to Make Your Team, Your Clients, and Your Boss Happy

In Chapter 8 we learned what makes people happy or unhappy. But what can be done in our organization to make us and people around us happy?

1.   **Always make sure that people get something more for their work than they had before**. Remember the increment and accumulation laws from Chapter 8? Recall, if you do have to reduce compensation or perks, it will make your team members very unhappy, often completely out of proportion to the reduction. If you are thinking about trying to save money by removing the coffee machine in the lunch room, think carefully about how much you will save: saving a couple of hundred dollars on a relatively cheap benefit may cost you magnitudes more in lost productivity from your unhappy team. For the same reason, continuous increases in salary or other measureable benefits are important. If there are

no funds available, even a small increment in perks will satisfy most people and maintain their level of happiness. A $20–$50 gift certificate every quarter may add the same amount of happiness as a small, but more expensive, salary increase. The amounts we are discussing here are really quite trivial, but companies tend to ignore this simple rule because of an illusion: it is much easier to count money saved than to calculate money lost due to lost productivity.

2.   **Avoid habituation**. In Chapter 8 we discussed habituation, where people's enjoyment of something decreases over a period of time. If you have a team member who has worked on the same type of projects for many years, their interest or enthusiasm is probably waning, regardless of how interesting the project may actually be. If you are a project manager, try to manage the project differently, better than the previous one. Also, try to assign people to different tasks and duties. Every member of your team will be happier.

3.   **Try to create memorable events**. Remember how time appears to go faster the longer we live? This is caused by routine and, if it continues unabated for years, we become unhappy. As a project manager, send your team member to a conference, ask them to write a paper for a journal, or ask them to do a client presentation – anything that would break the routine and create a memorable event. Even a simple lunch or other team-building events will help you out in this regard.

4.   **Properly manage expectations**. Do not tell your manager that you can do work faster than is realistically possible. Any discrepancy between expectation and reality makes people unhappy. Do not promise that the snow removal machine you are designing will also clean the sidewalk (unless of course it can); instead, say that the chance that the sidewalk will be cleaner will increase. By using "probabilistic language," you will be more accurate, manage expectations, and everyone will be happier with the final product.

What to Do to Make Yourself Happy and Spread the Virus of Happiness

By now it should be clear that organizational engineering is really about happiness. The goal is to "engineer" a happy project team. Happy project teams are highly correlated with successful projects. If you remember from Chapter 8, 50% of our own happiness is completely dependent upon our genetic inheritance. But that means that 50% isn't and you can do something to increase your happiness (Lyubomirsky et al. 2005; Moskowitz 2010).

1. **Be grateful and say nice things to your team members**. People who were asked to write letters of gratitude to other people reported a lasting increase in happiness – extending over weeks and even months – after implementing the habit. Interestingly, sending the letter was not necessary; even when people wrote letters but never delivered them, they still reported better feeling.

2. **Start imagining a better future and write it down**. If you start imagining a better future – for example, living with a loving partner, having a good job – and then leave a strong imprint of this imagination in your memory, you will begin to feel better. Writing down your vision of a happy future will create a much stronger impression and have a greater positive effect on your happiness.

3. **Write down three good things that have happened with you every week**. If you focus on the positive, it will help you to remember reasons to be glad.

4. **Help somebody else**. Helping someone else will boost your own happiness and vice versa. Executives that have to fire somebody are usually much less happy than a project engineer who spent some extra time helping their colleagues to learn a new skill.

In Chapter 8 we learned that happiness can act like a virus that can spread throughout a social group, including your project team. As a project manager, if you are able to make yourself happy, you can "infect" the rest of your team. Therefore your own feelings are not a completely private matter: your happiness may be the key to your project team's success.

SMART TIPS

The dominant corporate culture found in most large businesses leads to employee disengagement and, as a result, loss of company productivity. Choice engineering can help to alleviate this problem. Key strategies include:

- Disclosure therapy – provide clear information about the business in a clear format where an individual would see that project success is attributed to their personal efforts.
- Incremental improvement – make sure that your team members receive an incremental increase in monetary or non-monetary compensation.
- Stay happy yourself and spread the virus of happiness in your organization.

Conclusions

It is amazing how often people are affected by illusions and the significant consequences of these illusions. People spend enormous efforts to acquire the trappings of wealth – a large house, a new car, a trophy wife, etc. – because of the illusion that it will bring them happiness, but it does not. People start wars because of the illusion that they will be better off, but it makes their lives worse. Amazingly, most people are aware that these are illusions, but they are still entrapped in them.

Similarly, we can see this phenomenon in project management. In this book we have provided many examples of illusions that can affect the way in which we plan and execute projects: from the illusion of control to overconfidence, from the optimism and planning fallacy to the sunk cost effect. Here is a final one (*AFP News* 2009). Early in December 2009, people across Norway were witness to a series of mysterious spiraling blue lights that sparked rumors of UFOs. In fact, the spiral was quite spectacular and was visible for several hours in the night sky. It left thousands of residents in the north of the country baffled. Unfortunately, it wasn't a UFO (as that would be very exciting); it was the fallout from a failed test of Russia's new, submarine-based intercontinental missile, the Bulava. What is more remarkable was this missile failure was the result of a different kind of mental mistake: this time related to project management. From 2004 to 2009, the Bulava failed 7 of 13 tests (RIA Novosti 2012). Despite enormous efforts by Russian engineers, the missile was not operational until 2012. The nuclear submarines that were built to carry and launch these missiles are already operational, but without these missiles, they are just extremely expensive submersibles. Experts believe that the primary reason behind the Bulava failures is the inability of Russian defense contractors to manage the complex projects required to produce these types of weapons.

The complexity of many projects in many industries has grown exponentially over the last few decades. Projects include multiple external contractors and suppliers, often in different countries, very complex designs, and a growing number of risks, including financial, quality, public relations, environmental, and others. But many project managers, executives, and policymakers are still under the illusion that they can manage the project using traditional methods.

The world has changed, but people continue and will continue to make predictable and repeatable mental mistakes. It is the way we are hardwired. These mental mistakes and illusions impose significant burdens on everybody. Here are our suggestions to lessen these burdens:

- Learn about these mental mistakes; it will help you recognize and potentially mitigate the illusions they cause.

- Perform a structured analysis of project information and risks whenever possible.

- Use choice engineering to create an environment that encourages better decisions.

Appendix A: 14 Defenses against Project Illusions

Here are 14 tips to avoid the negative effect of illusions on your project and manage your project better. We believe that they are the most important ideas from this book. Detailed discussion of these ideas can be found throughout the book.

Table A.1   Fourteen tips to avoid the negative effect of illusions

	Think about Yourself		
1	Illusions vs Analysis **See Chapters 1 and 2.**	Regardless of how smart and experienced you are and the position you hold, always remember that your intuition has limitations and may lead to illusions. Analysis, which in most cases is simply logical thinking, will help you to make better decisions.	1. Use logic and analysis whenever possible, even when quick decisions are required. 2. Do not ignore project management analytical methods and tools: they are not a burden. Wrong decisions will end up costing you far more than you spend on these efforts.
2	The Zinedine Zidane Rule – named after the French soccer star whose emotional head-butt contributed to France's loss in the World Cup Finals. **See Chapter 5.**	High levels of stress or emotion can lead to poor decisions. More insidious, at times of high stress and emotion, most of us are unaware of the extent that emotions and stress are affecting the quality of our judgments.	1. Always have a cooling-off period between an event and a response. Ignore any impulses to make decisions until after the cooling-off period. 2. Plan a response to a potential crisis situation in advance. 3. Start meaningful and extensive discussion within a team if a crisis situation has occurred.

Table A.1   Fourteen tips to avoid the negative effect of illusions (*continued*)

3	Sunk Cost Rule – people try to defend previous choices: for example, they will continue to spend money in an attempt to recoup wasted investments. **See Chapter 6.**	When people make an incorrect decision, they often continue on the wrong course of action because they are afraid to admit a mistake or appear inconsistent. You can easily become entrapped if you try to be consistent for the sake of being consistent.	1. The ability to admit mistakes is a personal skill and should be encouraged to be part of your organization's culture. 2. The faster you reverse an incorrect decision or course of action, the less damage you will inflict on your projects.
4	Confirmation Rule – people tend to search and interpret new information in a way that confirms their preconceptions. For example, when you make a decision, you will use evidence that supports your position and ignore any that refutes it. **See Chapter 2.**	Very often our expectations affect our perceptions: we "see what we want to see." For instance, we do not recognize problems in our projects because they contradict our original plans.	1. Be honest about your motives and always seek the advice of others. 2. Always apply reality checks, independent assessment, various metrics and other techniques to ensure that you realistically interpret how your project performs.
5	*Better than Average Rule* – research found that 80% of respondents rated themselves in the top 30% of drivers. **See Chapter 2.**	People are more confident in their own behavior than they should be. *Overconfidence* leads to excessive risk-taking after a series of successes.	1. Always analyze what you can really do based on factual information, not on your perceptions. 2. If you do perform much better than average on your latest project, unless they are because of readily identifiable factors, like adoption of the agile methodology, it is very likely that the improved performance will be temporary and will trend back to its long-term average.
6	*Rule of Faulty Memory* – memory is not a storage chest in the brain into which we deposit some information and retrieve it later. Memories are reconstructed from both the original experience and related associations when we withdraw the information. **See Chapter 4.**	Memory is not perfect. We often remember the most remarkable or recent projects, but forget about the rest. Our years of successful work are often forgotten when someone makes a single mistake. Because of faulty memory people are making costly mistakes, for example underestimating the probability of certain events.	1. There are a few practical methods for managing information in your brain: use these methods to improve how accurately you memorize and recall information. 2. Project managers should be exposed to many different projects or learn about such projects in different industry events. 3. Create corporate knowledge base using simple off-the-shelf computer tools.

Table A.1   Fourteen tips to avoid the negative effect of illusions (*continued*)

Think about Your Project, Processes and Organization		
7	*Choice Engineering Rule – create processes or environments in which people would be steered towards making better choices rather than mandating these choices.* **See Chapter 3.**	Choice engineering is designed to gently push people towards making better choices without restricting these choices. An alternative to choice engineering is policing, which mandates certain processes and decisions.	1. Try to use choice engineering instead of or in addition to strict rules and regulations for your project. 2. In most projects there is certain space for both policing and choice engineering.
8	*Channel Tunnel Rule –* the project to design and construct the "Chunnel" under the English Channel that went significantly over budget. **See Chapters 1 and 2.**	Poor estimation and erroneous planning in project management is the result of two factors: *delusion* (psychological biases, such as optimism biases) and *deception* (deliberate errors made under organizational and political pressure).	1. To make better project estimates, try to mitigate cognitive biases by learning about potential mental pitfalls related to estimations. 2. Try to understand and eliminate motivational factors that affect estimates.
9	*Rule of Optimism –* everything you are trying to estimate in a project (duration, cost, resource usage, etc.) will be bigger than your original estimate, even if you are aware of this phenomenon. **See Chapter 2.**	Project managers often experience *optimism bias* or *planning fallacy*: people tend to see the future through "rose-colored glasses." It leads to wrong estimation and poor planning.	1. Always remember that intuitively you to tend to be overoptimistic: when you plan execution of a project, continue to ask the question, "What else can happen?" 2. Rely on historical data and quantitative tools rather than intuition to make estimation.
10	*"Don't be Evil" Rule –* named after the motto used in Google one of the best organizations to work for according to *Fortune Magazine*. **See Chapter 14.**	Many problems in projects occur due to disengaged project team members: people who do not share project goals cannot fully contribute to the project.	1. Always treat everybody involved in your project with respect, regardless of their role in the project, position, pay grade, etc. 2. Give people everything you can, even if you think that it may not be necessary or too much: it will eventually pay off.
11	*Rule of Adaptive Management* **See Chapter 12.**	The best project plans do not guarantee a good result. Successful organizations actively improve and revise plans by learning from outcomes of decisions previously taken.	1. Do not try to define everything in your project up front: iterative project execution may be the best way to go. 2. Always collect lessons learned, analyze them, and apply them to future projects.

Table A.1   Fourteen tips to avoid the negative effect of illusions
**   (*continued*)**

12	*Status Quo Rule* – a common bias often used by politicians: they convince voters that, if things are not so bad, there is no need to look for better government. **See Chapter 12.**	Status quo is not always the best solution; however, people are often scared of change, "better the devil you know than the one you don't," so will opt for the status quo when the situation is not dire. Remember, even if business is not bad, it does not mean that it cannot be improved.	1. Establish an organizational culture where current technology and project management processes are regularly reviewed and improved as needed. 2. Always support and try to implement innovative ideas in your project team.
13	*Rule of Increments* – people's perceived level of happiness is based on the feeling that they are regularly receiving incremental improvements in their lives. **See Chapter 8.**	Only happy people can fully contribute to a project. Happiness increases when we earn or receive something that is an improvement upon what we currently have. Happiness can spread like a virus across social networks; this includes project teams.	1. To ensure that people are happy in your project team, always try to give them more than they had before. 2. Be happy yourself and try to contribute in spreading happiness in your team.
14	*Expected Value Rule* – expected value is a probability-weighted average of all outcomes. **See Chapter 10.**	Expected value is an easy-to-use method to select the best course of action for your projects. Decisions are made by comparing the expected value of different scenarios.	1. Try to apply expected value when you assess multiple scenarios under uncertainties. 2. Be careful in estimating probabilities; it may cause a significant mistake in your analysis.

Appendix B:
Heuristics, Biases, Traps, and Other Psychological Effects in Project Management

While this is not a comprehensive list, we believe that we have captured the most relevant heuristics and biases that apply to project management. The biases are presented in alphabetical order. A few fundamental psychological concepts, such as selection perception and some heuristics, have a number of biases associated with them. Not all heuristics and biases are discussed in this book directly.

Ambiguity effect – people prefer alternatives where probabilities are known and avoid alternatives where the probability seems to be "unknown" (Ellsberg 1961). "Unknown" probabilities most often occur when certain information is missing or incomplete. Therefore, in project management, it is important to consistently collect information about all project alternatives before making important project decisions (see Chapter 9).

Anchoring heuristic – people rely on a piece of information when making decisions. For more information, see Chapter 7. Here are biases related to the anchoring heuristic:

> **Insufficient adjustment** – people "anchor" on a current value and make insufficient adjustments for future effects. Project managers do not allow sufficient adjustment after making estimations: for example, estimation of an activity's duration or cost.

Overconfidence in estimation of probabilities – people are often overly optimistic with their estimates of uncertain events. People often set ranges of probability too low and remain overconfident that these ranges will include true values. Overconfidence is most likely after a series of project successes and can lead to risk-taking. See Chapter 2 for more information.

Overestimating the probability of conjunctive events – if an event comprises a number of elementary events, the probability of elementary events should be multiplied to come up with the probability of the main event. For example, the probability of success for the particular activity is 80%. If there are three activities, the probability will be (0.8 x 0.8 x 0.8) 51.2%. See Chapter 11 for more information.

Ascription of causality – people ascribe causation even when the evidence only suggests correlation. For example, project managers believe that a project succeeded because they created and managed a project schedule. There is a correlation between project success rate and the presence of a project schedule, but it is not enough to make a judgment that a project schedule leads to this positive result.

Attribution biases – attribution is the way we determine who or what was responsible for an event or action. Attribution biases include:

Egocentric bias – people claim more responsibility for themselves for the results of a joint action than an outside observer would. In project teams, members often believe that they deserve more recognition than other team members.

False consensus effect – team members often overestimate the degree to which others agree with them. If members of a group reach a consensus and it is not disputed, they tend to believe that everybody thinks the same way (Ross et al. 1977). Therefore, if nobody expresses a contrary opinion in a project team meeting, project managers will believe that everybody agrees on the course of actions.

Outgroup homogeneity bias – people see members of their own team as being relatively more varied than members of other groups.

Self-fulfilling prophecy – a false statement (prophecy) that may push people to take actions that will ultimately result in fulfillment of the prophecy (Merton 1968). For example, a project manager expresses a concern about the low quality of supplies. He performs an unusually detailed quality control and actually finds some problems which otherwise would not be discovered.

Self-serving bias – people claim responsibility for successes rather than failures, which results in overconfidence. For example, project managers of a successfully completed project might say, "Our team achieved this due to our good management practices." If a project fails, the manager could say: "Clients did not provide clear specifications."

Trait ascription bias – people view themselves as relatively variable in terms of behavior, intellect, or emotions while viewing others as much more predictable. It is because people are able to observe and understand themselves better than others. This bias may lead to stereotypes and prejudice in project teams.

Availability heuristic – people make judgments about the probability of the occurrence of events by how easily these events are brought to mind. See Chapter 7 for more information. Here are biases related to the availability heuristic:

Illusory correlations – people overestimate the frequency with which two events occur together. If a project manager analyses the relationships between two or more parameters – for example the geographic location of a supplier related to the quality of their product – the assessment could be wrong.

Vividness – people easier recall events that are unusual, rare, vivid, or associated with other events, such as major issues, successes, or failures. Ease of recall of certain events may not be associated with the actual probability of the event. In project management, assessment of probabilities for project events including risks can be wrong.

Bandwagon effect (groupthink) – people have some beliefs or have certain behaviors because many other people have similar beliefs or behaviors. Project managers and team members are often reluctant to express different points of view.

Bias blind spot – people don't recognize their own cognitive biases (Pronin et al. 2002). Even if people can recognize their own mental mistakes, they tend not to mitigate their negative effect. This bias emphasizes the importance of learning psychological aspects for project management.

Choice-supportive bias – people remember positive attributes as having been part of the chosen option than of the rejected option. For example, people were asked to make a choice between two options. Later, in a memory test, participants were given a list of positive and negative features. Positive features were more likely to be attributed to the chosen option and negative features are more likely to be attributed to the rejected option (Mather and Johnson 2000). This bias is related to **self-serving bias**.

Collective trap – if a number of people with different agendas interact but do not necessarily fully communicate with each other, they may come to irrational conclusions or decisions (Plous 1993). The relationships between customers and developers often lead to collective traps when both sides do not clearly state their expectations (Chapter 6).

Context effect – memory is dependent on the context of the environment. Out-of-context memories are more difficult to retrieve than in-context memories. For example, recall time and accuracy for a project-related memory will be lower at home than in the office. See Chapter 4 for more information about memory biases.

Deterioration trap – people have taken a certain course of action, but over time when conditions changed, what initially seemed to be a good decision turns out to be irrational. This trap is related to **time delay trap**. See Chapter 6 for more information.

Disconfirmation bias – people are usually more critical of information that contradicts their prior beliefs (Lord et al. 1979). This bias is related to the **confirmation bias**. For example, if a project manager believes that a supplier may delay the delivery of the component, he or she will apply more than usual scrutiny analyzing the performance of this supplier.

Dread factor – people tend to be less concerned about risks that are not catastrophic, but are controllable and are easily reduced. This factor affects risk attitude (Slovic 1987). Read about this factor in Chapter 11.

Endowment effect – people place a higher value on objects they own relative to objects they do not. It explains why people rarely exchange a product they have already purchased for a better product. Project managers often prefer not to replace existing products, tools, and services (Kahneman et al. 1991).

Experiential limitations – people don't look beyond the scope of past experiences and reject unfamiliar facts. Project managers may discard good ideas because they do not fit a familiar pattern.

Exposure effect – people may like certain things because they are familiar with them. The more often we read about a certain product, method, or principle, the more we like it. For example, a project manager may like certain project management software just because it is advertised more often in an industry journal. Exposure effect belongs to memory biases and effects. See Chapter 4 for more information about memory biases.

Failure to consider alternatives – people often consider only one alternative or scenario. Project managers often plan a project based on evaluation of one project alternative.

False memory – a memory of an event that did not happen or a distortion of an event that did occur. See more information about memory biases in Chapter 4.

Focusing effect – people often place too much importance on one aspect of an event. For example, a project manager believes that a software project's duration mostly depends on resource availability and requests more resources. In reality, project duration depends on many factors, including team collaboration, qualification of personnel, etc.

Generation effect – people will recall information better if they experience it rather than simply read about it. If a project manager experienced a certain issue, such as project delay or cost overrun and actually dealt with it, he or she will remember it better than just reading about it. The generation effect can be a strategy for learning (Jacoby 1978). Generation effect belongs to memory biases and effects.

Groupthink – *see* **Bandwagon effect**.

Hindsight bias (I-knew-it-all-along effect) – people see past events as being more predictable than they actually were. For example, if a project manager evaluates past project failures, he or she believes that the potential failures could be easily identified before the project started. The possible explanation of this bias is that events that actually occur are easier to recall than possible outcomes which did not occur.

Hyperbolic discounting – people prefer smaller payoffs to larger payoffs when the smaller payoffs come sooner in time than the larger payoffs. As a result, project managers may underestimate long-term opportunities and overestimate short-term opportunities. For instance, a project manager may prefer a $500,000 project revenue now than one with a $1 million revenue several years from now. However, given the choice of the same $500,000 project revenue five years from now and the $1 million six years from now, project managers would choose $1 million in six years (Chung and Herrnstein 1967).

Illusion of control – people believe that they are in control of a situation when in fact they are not. For example, when rolling dice in craps, people tend to throw stronger for high numbers and softer for low numbers. Illusion of control can cause unrealistic optimism in project managers. See Chapter 11 for more information.

Impact bias – people believe that if a negative event occurs, it takes longer to recover from the event than it actually does. In project management it is related to the analysis of risk impacts.

Inconsistency – people often apply different criteria or make different decisions in similar situations. Inconsistencies lead to irrational choices. Project managers may apply different analysis of project cost on similar projects. This effect is opposite to **tendency to be consistent**.

Inertia – people prefer not to change thought patterns that they have used in the past in the face of new circumstances or environment. Project managers often follow the same practices in a new environment, such as project size, industry, organizational structure, etc.

Information bias – people often try to get information even when it cannot affect a decision. In organizations, management sometimes requires more reports and results of analysis than necessary. See Chapter 9 for more on managing information in project management.

Invisible correlations – people don't see correlations between events of processes because they do not seem to be related. In project management, this is often related to correlation between individuals' motivation, beliefs, experience, and preferences and project results. Correlation between corporate culture, happiness and project results are often overlooked. See Chapter 14 for more information.

Loss aversion – people prefer avoiding losses versus acquiring gains (Kahneman and Tversky 1979). In other words, people are willing to take more risks when they are going to lose something. In project management it is associated with risk aversion and risk tolerance when decision-makers evaluate possible project gains and losses. Read about loss aversion in Chapter 11 of this book.

Misinformation effect – the memory of the event is affected by environment or circumstances when the event is recalled. If people read an inaccurate report about their own project and are asked to recall their own experience about the project, the report will distort their memory about the project (Roediger et al. 2001). Read Chapter 4 about memory biases.

Omission bias – people judge potentially harmful actions as worse than equally harmful inactions (omissions). Project managers may believe that new product development is riskier than continuing to maintain an old existing product that is losing sales, even if the cost of both project alternatives is the same. This bias is related to **status quo bias**.

Optimism bias – people are usually overoptimistic about the outcome of planned actions. Project managers often overestimate the probability of a successful project completion and underestimate the probability of negative events or risks. The optimism bias is also related to **wishful thinking** and **planning fallacy**. Read more about optimism bias in Chapter 2.

Outcome bias – people evaluate an original decision by its final outcome instead of based on the quality of the decision at the time it was made. If a decision results in a negative outcome, this does not mean that the decision was wrong, because the decision was made based on the best possible information at the time.

Overconfidence – see **overconfidence in estimation of probabilities**.

Peak-end rule – people judge their past experiences almost entirely on how they were at their peak (pleasant or unpleasant) and how they ended. Other information appears to be discarded, including net pleasantness or unpleasantness and how long the experience lasted (Kahneman 1999). See Chapter 9 for more information. Biases related to peak-end rule heuristic include:

> **Rosy retrospection** – people evaluate past events more positively than they actually rated them when the event occurred. This effect is often referred to as "the past is always well remembered" (Mitchell and Thompson 1994). The explanation may be that negative events fade from memory faster than positive events.

> **Zeigarnik effect** – people remember uncompleted or interrupted tasks better than completed ones (Zeigarnik 1967). In other words, remembering something is easy when study is interrupted.

Picture superiority effect – concepts and ideas are much more likely to be remembered if they are presented as pictures rather than as words (Paivio 1971, 1986). Project information is easier to present and interpret if it is presented graphically. The effect is related to **availability heuristic** (**vividness**). Read Chapter 9 regarding project information.

Planning fallacy – people underestimate the duration of activities. For example, project managers may eliminate factors that they perceive are not related to the project. Moreover, project managers may discount multiple improbable high-impact risks because each one is unlikely to happen. The planning fallacy is related to **optimism bias**.

Polarization effect – group discussions may lead to amplified preferences of group members. If a project team member already has an opinion about a certain issue (for example product requirements), as a result of the meeting, he or she may have a much stronger opinion about this issue (Lord et al. 1979).

Post-purchase rationalization – when people have invested a lot of time, money, or effort in something, they try to convince themselves that the efforts must have been worth it. This bias is related to **sunk cost effect**.

Prudence trap – unrealistic assessment of the probabilities of future events may lead to project planning based on the worst case scenario. It may cause major losses. Read more about this and other behavioral traps in Chapter 6.

Pseudocertainty effect – people make risk-averse choices if the expected outcome is positive, but make risk-seeking choices to avoid negative outcomes (Tversky and Kahneman 1981; Slovic et al. 1982). Project managers will prefer to take a risk and buy a component if they receive a free unit for every three purchased instead of buying all four components with 25% discount. See Chapter 11 for more information.

Publication bias – people have a tendency to report results that confirm expectations differently from results that are negative or inconclusive. This is a very common phenomenon in research and development projects. Negative results or results which do not confirm the original hypothesis are also valuable and should be reported in the same manner as positive results (Chapter 7).

Recognition heuristic – when people select an alternative they select an item which is recognized. The recognized item will be considered to have a higher criterion value (Goldstein and Gigerenzer 1999). Project managers select project alternatives which are familiar to them, but not necessarily the best alternative.

Representativeness heuristic – people estimate probability by judging how representative the object, person, or event is of a category, group, or process. For more information about this heuristic see Chapter 7. Here are biases related to the representativeness heuristic:

> **Conjunction fallacy** – an unwanted appeal to more detailed scenarios. This fallacy can lead to a "preference for details": if project managers must select one project from a number of proposals, he or she may tend to pick those proposals with the most detail, even though they may not have the best chance of success.

> **Gambler's fallacy** – people's belief that a successful outcome is due after a run of bad luck (Tversky and Kahneman 1971). In project management, corrective actions as a response to certain issues and problems are often not taken because project managers believe that the situation will improve by itself. Read about this fallacy in Chapter 11.

Hot hand fallacy – a gambler has had a streak of luck. Therefore, the gambler is either "hot" or "cold," depending on whether his luck is good or bad and the good or bad luck will continue at a probability greater than chance. This fallacy is similar to **gambler's fallacy**.

Ignoring base-rate frequencies – people ignore prior statistical information (base-rate frequencies) when making assessments about probabilities. For example, what is the probability that a new component is defective? Project managers can make estimates based on recent testing where most components were defective. However, he or she may ignore the fact that historically 99% of the components from this supplier have been problem-free (Chapter 7).

Ignoring regression to mean – people expect extreme events to be followed by similar extreme events. In reality, extreme events most likely will be followed by an extreme in the opposite way or an average event. Project managers should not expect extraordinary performances from a team or individuals for every project because of the regression to mean or tendency to be average.

Selective perception – people's expectations affect their perception. Sometimes selective perception is referred to as "what I see is what I want to see." Here are biases related to selective perception:

Confirmation bias – people actively seek out and assign more weight to evidence that confirms their hypothesis, and ignore or underweight evidence that could discount their hypothesis (Watson 1960). For more information see Chapter 2.

Premature termination of search for evidence – people often accept the first or one of the first explanations of an event that apparently might work. If there is a project failure, project managers often stop looking for root causes after finding some simple explanation. This bias is related to **failure to consider alternatives**.

Professional viewpoint effect – people look at something according to the conventions of their profession, forgetting any broader point of view. For example, project engineers may look at a project from an engineering point of view and disregard project management methodologies and tools.

Similarity heuristic – people make their judgments based on similarity. Project managers usually analyze project issues by comparing these issues with previously corrected problems. Over time, a project manager's past experiences will allow their use of the similarity heuristic to be highly effective, quickly choosing the corrective actions that will likely reveal the problem's source.

Source credibility bias – people reject information if there is a bias against the person, organization, or group to which the person belongs. The opposite effect is the tendency to accept information from trusted sources. In project management it can lead to a sampling bias, when too much faith is placed in certain information while other information is rejected (Skinner 2009).

Status quo bias – people like things to stay relatively the same (Samuelson and Zeckhauser 1988). This bias is similar to the **omission bias** and is related to **endowment effect**. This bias explains why ineffective project management procedures often are not changed and why outdated technology is not replaced. For more information see Chapter 12.

Sunk cost effect – people make choices considering the cost and effort that has already been incurred and cannot be recovered (sunk cost). Sunk costs affect decisions due to **loss aversion** effect. Sunk costs may cause cost overruns and may also lead to an investment in a project that now has no value. See Chapter 6 for more information.

Tendency to be consistent – people become uncomfortable if they are accused of being inconsistent. For more information see Chapter 12.

Time delay trap – people don't think about the long-term consequences of their decisions. People often take the "buy now – pay later" option to discover that they cannot afford whatever they bought. Read Chapter 6 for more information.

Unknown factor – people are less concerned about risks that are observable, have immediate effects, and are known to science. This factor affects people's attitude toward risk. Read about this factor in Chapter 11.

Unrealistic optimism – people believe that negative events are more likely to happen to other people and positive events are more likely to happen to them. See also **optimism bias** or **planning fallacy**. See Chapter 11 for more information.

Wishful thinking – people believe what might be pleasing to imagine instead of by appealing to evidence or rationality. For example, a project manager often makes estimates based on positive results he or she wants to achieve instead of what is possible to achieve. Wishful thinking is related to the **optimism bias**.

Zero-risk bias (related to **certainty effect**) – people prefer to reduce probability and impact of a small risk to zero rather than effect a greater reduction to a larger risk. People may prefer small benefits that are certain to large ones that are uncertain. Project managers sometimes prefer to avoid risk completely rather than significantly mitigate it. For more information see Chapter 13.

Appendix C: Risk and Decision Analysis Software

Below is a list of risk and decision analysis software products used in project management. All software within a category is listed in alphabetical order.

Table C.1   Quantitative project risk analysis software

Product Name	Company	Comments
@RISK for Project	Palisade Corporation 798 Cascadilla Street Ithaca, NY 14850, USA www.palisade.com	Quantitative risk analysis for Microsoft® Project.
Full Monte Carlo	Barbecana 1001 S. Dairy Ashford, Ste 100 Houston, TX 77077 +1 713-595-6688 www. barbecana.com	Quantitative risk analysis for Microsoft® Project.
Primavera Risk Analysis	Oracle Corporation 500 Oracle Parkway Redwood Shores, CA 94065, USA www.oracle.com	Quantitative risk analysis for Oracle's Primavera®.
RiskyProject	Intaver Institute Inc. 303, 6707, Elbow Drive S.W., Calgary, Alberta, T2V0E5, Canada www.intaver.com	Quantitative risk analysis: works standalone, as well as with Microsoft® Project, Oracle's Primavera® and other project management software.

Table C.2   Enterprise risk management software

Product Name	Company	Comments
Active Risk	Active Risk Group 1 Grenfell Road Maidenhead, Berks SL6 1HN, UK www.activerisk.com/	Web-based enterprise risk management including qualitative and quantitative risk analysis.
Enterprise Risk Register	Incom Pty Ltd 8 Normac St, Roseville, NSW, Australia. 2069 www.incom.com.au	Web-based enterprise project risk management software.
Iris Intelligence	Iris Intelligence Ltd. 100 Pall Mall, London SW1Y 5HP, UK www.irisintelligence.com	Web-based enterprise risk management including qualitative and quantitative risk analysis.
Primavera Risk Analysis	Oracle Corporation 500 Oracle Parkway Redwood Shores, CA 94065, USA www.oracle.com	Enterprise-level project risk management software. Includes qualitative and quantitative risk analysis and risk register.
Predict!	Risk Decisions Limited Whichford House, Parkway Court, Oxford Business Park South, Oxford OX4 2JY, UK www.riskdecisions.com	Integrated enterprise risk management and risk analysis software.
RiskExchange	Saber Systems Inc. 65 W. Street Road Suite A-200, P.O. Box 3417 Warminster, PA 18974, USA www.sabresystems.com	Web-based risk management software.
RiskyProject Enterprise	Intaver Institute Inc. 303, 6707, Elbow Drive S.W., Calgary, Alberta, Canada, T2V0E5 www.intaver.com	Quantitative and qualitative enterprise risk analysis and risk management software.

Table C.3   Brainstorming software used in project management

Product Name	Company	Comment
MindManager	MindJet Corporation 1160 Battery Street, 4th Floor San Francisco, CA 94111, USA www.mindjet.com	Visual tools for brainstorming ideas, strategic thinking, and information management.
MindMapper	SimTech Systems USA 1565 W. Main St. Suite 208-310 Lewisville, TX 75067, USA www.mindmapper.com	Visual tool for brainstorming and information management.

Table C.3 Brainstorming software used in project management (*continued*)

Product Name	Company	Comment
MindView	MatchWare Inc. 311 South Brevard Avenue Tampa, FL 33606-2205, USA www.matchware.com	Productivity software for capturing, organizing, developing and presenting information.
PathMaker	SkyMark Corporation 7300 Penn Avenue Pittsburgh, PA 15208, USA www.skymark.com	Strategy planning, brainstorming, process improvement, meeting management, quality management and data analysis.
Project KickStart	Experience in Software 2029 Durant Ave. Berkeley, CA 94704, USA www.projectkickstart.com	Project initialization and planning software.
SmartDraw	SmartDraw.com 9909 Mira Mesa Blvd., San Diego, CA 92131, USA www.smartdraw.com	Business graphics and mind mapping software.

Table C.4 Other Decision and Risk Analysis Software Used in Project Management

Product Name	Company	Comment
Analytica	Lumina Decision Systems, Inc. 26010 Highland Way Los Gatos, CA 95033-9758, USA www.lumina.com	Visual tool for creating, analyzing, and communicating decision models. Economic model of the project is created using influence diagrams.
Crystal Ball	Oracle Corporation 500 Oracle Parkway Redwood Shores, CA 94065, USA www.oracle.com	Risk analysis for spreadsheets.
Decision Explorer	Banxia Software 141 Highgate, Kendal, Cumbria, LA9 4EN, UK www.banxia.com	Qualitative problem structuring.
Decision Lens Suite and Decision Lens Web	Decision Lens 4250 North Fairfax Dr., Suite 1410, Arlington, VA 22203 www.decisionlens.com	Modeling and decision analysis software. Include multi-criteria decision-making functionalities.
DecisionTools Suite	Palisade Corporation 798 Cascadilla Street Ithaca, NY 14850, USA www.palisade.com	Includes @RISK risk analysis software with spreadsheets, decision tree analysis, sensitivity analysis, optimization, distribution fitting, and visualization tools.

Table C.4   Other Decision and Risk Analysis Software Used in Project Management (*continued*)

Product Name	Company	Comment
DTrio Owl TreeTop	Decision Frameworks LP 9821 Katy Freeway, Suite 550 Houston, TX 77024, USA	Software which supports corporate decision process.
DPL	Syncopation Software, Inc. 1623 Main Street Concord, MA 01742, USA www.syncopation.com	Desktop tool for decision analysis and real option valuation. Includes influence diagrams, decision tree analysis, Monte Carlo simulation, and sensitivity analysis.
Expert Choice	Expert Choice 2111 Wilson Bvld. Suite 763 Arlington, VA 22201, USA www.expertchoice.com	Enterprise-level collaboration and decision-support software. Includes multi-criteria decision-making functionalities.
RiskTrak	RiskTrak International 101 State Route 101A, Suite #101 Amherst, NH 03031-2274, USA www.risktrak.com	Windows-based risk management software.
SmartOrg products: Project Navigator, Portfolio Navigator, Decision Advisor Supertree/ Sensitivity	SmartOrg, Inc. 855 Oak Grove Avenue, Suite 202 Menlo Park, CA 94025, USA www.smartorg.net	Modeling, evaluating, forecasting and managing the business opportunities in projects and portfolios; decision tree and sensitivity analysis.
Spotfire Products: Spotfire, DecisionSite Analytics Server Spotfire S+	TIBCO Software Inc. 3303 Hillview Avenue Palo Alto, CA 94304, USA www.spotfire.com	Business data analysis and visualization software.
Tableau	Tableau Software 837 North 34th Street, Suite 400 Seattle, WA 98103, USA www.tableausoftware.com	Data visualization and business intelligence software.
TreeAge Pro	TreeAge Software, Inc. 1075 Main Street Williamstown, MA 01267, USA www.treeage.com	Decision tree and influence diagram, sensitivity analysis, Bayes' revision, Monte Carlo simulation and multi-attribute analysis.
Vanguard Products: Decision Tree Suite, Business Analytics Suite, Knowledge Automation System, and Vanguard System	Vanguard Software Corp. 1100 Crescent Green Cary, NC 27518, USA www.vanguardsw.com	Forecasting, decision tree analysis, Monte Carlo simulation, optimization, time series forecasting, and expert systems.

Note: Microsoft is a registered trademark of Microsoft Corporation in the United States and/or other countries. Primavera® is a registered trademark of Oracle Corporation. All other names and trademarks are the property of their respective owners.

Appendix D: Professional Associations, Societies, and Groups in the Area of Risk and Decision Analysis

American Economic Association – http://www.vanderbilt.edu/AEA/

American Risk and Insurance Association – http://www.aria.org/.

American Statistical Association Section on Bayesian Statistical Science – http://community.amstat.org/SBSS/Home.

American Statistical Association Section on Risk Analysis – http://www.amstat.org/sections/srisk/.

Association for the Advancement of Cost Engineering (AACEI) – http://www.aacei.org.

Association for Uncertainty in Artificial Intelligence – http://www.auai.org/.

College of Scheduling of Project Management Institute – http://www.pmicos.org/.

Decision Analysis Society in INFORMS (DAS) – http://decision-analysis.society.informs.org/.

Decision Sciences Institute – http://www.decisionsciences.org/.

European Association of Decision Making (EADM) – http://www.eadm.eu/.

European Association of Operational Research Societies (EURO) – http://www.euro-online.org/.

Game Theory Society – http://www.gametheorysociety.org/.

Institute for Operations Research and the Management Sciences (INFORMS) – http://www.informs.org/.

International Society for Bayesian Analysis (ISBA) – http://www.bayesian.org/.

International Society for Multi-Criteria Decision Making (MCDM) – http://www.mcdmsociety.org/.

Public Choice Society – http://www.publicchoicesociety.org/.

Risk Management Special Interest Group (RiskSIG) – http://www.risksig.com/.

Society for Imprecise Probabilities and Their Applications (SIPTA) – http://www.sipta.org/.

Society for Judgment and Decision-Making (JDM) – http://www.sjdm.org/.

Society for Mathematical Psychology (SMP) – http://aris.ss.uci.edu/smp/index.html.

Society for Medical Decision Making (SMDM) – http://www.smdm.org/.

Society for Neuroeconomics – http://www.neuroeconomics.org/.

Society for Risk Analysis – http://www.sra.org/.

Appendix E: Decision and Risk Analysis Journals

Journals Published by INFORMS

INFORMS publications: http://www2.informs.org/Pubs/

Decision Analysis (http://da.pubs.informs.org/)
Decision Analysis is dedicated to advancing the theory, application, and teaching of all aspects of decision analysis. The *Decision Analysis* audience includes anyone interested in the practical aspects of decision analysis and decision theory.

Management Science (http://mansci.pubs.informs.org/)
Management Science is a scholarly journal that publishes scientific research into the problems, interests, and concerns of managers. This includes decision and risk analysis.

Operations Research (http://www3.informs.org/site/OperationsResearch/)
Operations Research publishes papers related to different areas of operations research including decision and risk analysis. The journal serves the entire operations research community, including practitioners, researchers, educators, and students.

Organizational Science (http://www3.informs.org/site/Organization_Science/)
Organization Science publishes fundamental research about organizations, including their processes, structures, technologies, identities, capabilities, forms, and performance. It includes applications of decision and risk.

Interfaces (http://interfaces.pubs.informs.org/)
Interfaces, a bimonthly journal of INFORMS, is dedicated to improving the practical application of OR/MS to decisions and policies in today's organizations and industries.

Journal Published by the Society for Judgment and Decision Making (SJDM)

Judgment and Decision Making (http://journal.sjdm.org/)
The journal publishes scholarly articles that deal with normative, descriptive, and/or prescriptive analyses of human judgments and decisions.

Journal Published by Project Management Institute (PMI)

Project Management Journal (http://www.pmi.org/en/Knowledge-Center/Publications-Project-Management-Journal.aspx))
Project Management is a quarterly refereed journal containing advanced, state-of-the-art project management techniques, research, theories, and applications.

Journals Published by Wiley

Wiley Publications: http://www3.interscience.wiley.com/cgi-bin/home.

Journal of Behavioral Decision Making (http://www3.interscience.wiley.com/cgi-bin/jhome/4637/)
The journal publishes original empirical reports, critical review papers, theoretical analyses, and methodological contributions. The journal also features book, software, and decision-aiding technique reviews.

Journal of Forecasting (http://www3.interscience.wiley.com/cgi-bin/jhome/2966/)
The multidisciplinary journal publishes papers dealing with any aspect of forecasting: theoretical, practical, computational, and methodological.

Journal of Multi-Criteria Decision Analysis (http://www3.interscience.wiley.com/cgi-bin/jhome/5725/)
The journal provides an international forum for the presentation and discussion of all aspects of research, application, and evaluation of multi-criteria decision

analysis. Papers address mathematical, theoretical, and behavioral aspects of decision analysis.

Journals Published by Springer

Springer Publications: http://www.springer.com.

Group Decision and Negotiation (http://www.springerlink.com/content/1572-9907/) The journal publishes papers concerning unifying approaches to group decision and negotiation processes.

Journal of Happiness Studies (http://www.springer.com/sociology/well-being/journal/10902)
Journal of Happiness Studies is devoted to scientific understanding of subjective well-being. Coverage includes both cognitive evaluations of life, such as life satisfaction, and affective enjoyment of life, such as mood level.

Journal of Risk and Uncertainty (http://www.springerlink.com/content/1573-0476/) This journal is the natural outlet for the best research in decision analysis, economics, and psychology dealing with choice under uncertainty.

Theory and Decision (http://www.springer.com/economics/economic+theory/journal/11238)
Theory and Decision is an international journal for multidisciplinary advances in decision science.

Journals Published by Elsevier

Elsevier Publications: http://www.elsevier.com/wps/find/homepage.cws_home.

Decision Support Systems (http://www.elsevier.com/wps/find/journal description.cws_home/505540/description#description)
The journal publishes papers related to the concepts and operational basis for decision support systems (DSS), techniques for implementing and evaluating DSSs, DSS experiences, and related studies.

European Journal of Operational Research (http://www.elsevier.com/wps/find/
journaldescription.cws_home/505543/description#description)
The journal publishes papers on methodology of operational research and the
practice of decision-making.

Games and Economic Behavior (http://www.elsevier.com/wps/find/journal
description.cws_home/622836/description#description)
The journal facilitates cross-fertilization between theories and applications of
game theoretic reasoning.

International Journal of Forecasting (http://www.elsevier.com/wps/find/journal
description.cws_home/505555/description#description)
The journal publishes refereed papers covering all aspects of forecasting. It is
the official publication of the International Institute of Forecasters (IIF).

International Journal of Project Management (http://www.elsevier.com/wps/find/
journaldescription.cws_home/30435/description)
The journal offers wide-ranging and comprehensive coverage of all facets of
project management.

Journal of Mathematical Psychology (http://www.elsevier.com/wps/find/
journaldescription.cws_home/622887/description#description)
The journal publishes articles, monographs and reviews, notes and
commentaries, and book reviews in all areas of mathematical psychology.
Areas of special interest include fundamental measurement and psychological
process models, such as those based upon neural network or information
processing concepts.

Mathematical Social Sciences (http://www.elsevier.com/wps/find/journal
description.cws_home/505565/description#description)
The journal emphasizes the unity of mathematical modeling in economics,
psychology, political sciences, sociology, and other social sciences.

Other Publications

Blackwell Publishing: http://www.blackwell-synergy.com/.

Decision Sciences Journal (http://www.decisionsciences.org/dsj/)

Decision Sciences is a quarterly, professional journal that publishes papers related to the latest computer technology, mathematical and statistical techniques, and behavioral science.

References

Aamond, S. and Wang, S. 2007. Exercise on the Brain. *New York Times*. November 8.

AFP News Agency. 2009. New Russian Missile Fails Again in Test: Reports. Available online at http://www.google.com/hostednews/afp/article/ALeq M5hkj48C2Fl1IVRu2C_T_cY5DA0czQ (accessed September 12, 2011).

Alexander, K.L. 2009. Pants Hearing Rejected. *Washington Post*. March 3.

Amos, J. 2010. Obama Cancels Moon Return Project. *BBC News*. Available online at http://news.bbc.co.uk/2/hi/science/nature/8489097.stm (accessed September 12, 2011).

Andrews, G.S. 2009. *Canadian Professional Engineering and Geoscience: Practice and Ethics*. 4th edition. Mishawaka, IN: Nelson College Indigenous.

Ariely, D. 2009. *Predictably Irrational, Revised and Expanded Edition: The Hidden Forces That Shape Our Decisions*. New York: Harper.

Armor, D.A. and Taylor, S.E. 2002. When Predictions Fail: The Dilemma of Unrealistic Optimism. In T. Gilovich, D. Griffin and D. Kahneman (eds), *Heuristics and Biases: The Psychology of Intuitive Judgment*. Cambridge, UK: Cambridge University Press.

Baas, M., De Dreu, C.K.W. and Nijstad, B.A. 2008. A Meta-analysis of 25 Years of Mood-creativity Research: Hedonic Tone, Activation, or Regulatory Focus? *Psychological Bulletin* 134(6), 779–806.

Barron, J. 1983. *Mig Pilot: The Final Escape of Lt. Belenko*. New York: Avon Books.

Baucells, M. and Sarin, R.K. 2008a. The Mathematics of Happiness. In *Proceedings of INFORMS Annual Meeting*. Washington, DC. October 12–15.

Baucells, M. and Sarin, R.K. 2008b. Does More Money Buy You More Happiness? In T. Kugler, J.C. Smith, T. Connolly and Y. Son (eds), *Decision Modeling and Behavior in Complex and Uncertain Environments*. New York: Springer, 199–226.

BBC News. 2008. Fresh Baggage Woes at Terminal 5. Available online at http://news.bbc.co.uk/2/hi/uk_news/7331954.stm (accessed September 12, 2012).

BetterExplained. 2010. Understanding the Birthday Paradox. Available online
    at http://betterexplained.com/articles/understanding-the-birthday-paradox/
    (accessed September 12, 2012).

Blue Cross and Blue Shield of Michigan. 2010. Generic Drugs: Safe, Effective,
    FDA Approved. Available online at http://www.theunadvertisedbrand.com/
    (accessed September 12, 2012).

Bösch, H., Steinkamp, F. and Boller, E. 2006. Examining Psychokinesis: The
    Interaction of Human Intention with Random Number Generators – A Meta-
    analysis. *Psychological Bulletin* 132(4), 497–523.

Bourlioufas, N. 2007. Average Pay Packet Tops $57,000. News.com.au.
    November 15. Available online at http://www.news.com.au/business/male-
    pay-packets-near-61000/story-e6frfm1i-1111114883151 (accessed September
    12, 2012).

British Petroleum. 2012. BP Statistical Review of World Energy June 2012.
    Available online at www.bp.com/statisticalreview (accessed September 12,
    2012).

Browning, E.S. 2007. Exorcising Ghosts of Octobers Past. *The Wall Street
    Journal* October 15, C1–C2. Available online at http://online.wsj.com/
    article/SB119239926667758592.html?mod=mkts_main_news_hs_h
    (accessed September 12, 2012).

Bureau of Transportation Statistics. 2010. Number of U.S. Aircraft, Vehicles,
    Vessels, and Other Conveyances. Available online at http://www.bts.gov/
    publications/national_transportation_statistics/html/table_01_11.html
    (accessed September 12, 2012).

Buzan, T. and Buzan, B. 2010. *Mind Map Book: Unlock Your Creativity, Boost Your
    Memory, Change Your Life*. Upper Saddle River, NJ: Pearson Education Ltd.

CBC News. 2009. The Mackenzie Valley Pipeline. Available online at http://
    www.cbc.ca/news/business/story/2010/12/16/f-mackenzie-valley-pipeline-
    history.html (accessed September 12, 2012).

Center of Disease Control and Prevention (CDC). 2006. E. coli O157. Available
    online at http://www.cdc.gov/foodborne/ecolispinach/case_count_us_map.
    htm (accessed September 12, 2012).

Charette, R. 2005. Why Software Fails. IEEE Spectrum. September. Available
    online at http://spectrum.ieee.org/computing/software/why-software-fails/0
    (accessed September 12, 2012).

Chung, S.H. and Herrnstein, R.J. 1967. Choice and Delay of Reinforcement.
    Journal of Experimental Analysis of Behavior 10(1), 67–74.

Clemen, R.T. 1996. *Making Hard Decisions*. 2nd edition. Pacific Grove, CA:
    Brooks/Cole Publishing Company.

Clemen, R. and Kwit, R. 2001. The Value of Decision Analysis at Eastman Kodak Company, 1990–1999. *Interfaces* September/October, 74–92.

Committee of International Space Station Meteoroid/Debris Risk Management. 1997. *Protecting the Space Station from Meteoroids and Orbiting Debris.* Washington, DC: The National Academies Press.

Cropanzano, R. and Wright, T.A. 2001. When a "Happy" Worker is Really a Productive Worker: A Review and Further Refinement of the Happy-Productive Worker Thesis. *Consulting Psychology Journal: Practice and Research* 53, 182–99.

CTV News. 2010. O Canada Lyrics to be Reviewed. Available online at http://www.cbc.ca/arts/music/story/2010/03/03/o-canada-anthem.html (accessed September 12, 2012).

Demchenko, B., Krasikov, A., Teplykov, S. and Tumanova, I. 2009. Second Generator was Vibrating for 10 Years. *Izvestia* September 14.

Dog Bite Law. 2010. Dog Bite Law Statistics. Available online at http://www.dogbitelaw.com/PAGES/statistics.html (accessed September 12, 2012).

Economist. 2007. Playing Games with the Planet. September 27. Available online at http://www.economist.com/PrinterFriendly.cfm?story_id=9867020 (accessed September 12, 2012).

Ellsberg, D. 1961. Risk, Ambiguity, and the Savage Axioms. *Quarterly Journal of Economics* 75, 643–99.

Elstrom, P. 2002. How to Hide $3.8 Billion in Expenses. *Business Week* July 8.

Ermakova, M. 2007. Transcendental "Russia". *Rosiyskaya Gazeta* October 15.

Ert, E. and Erev, I. 2008. The Rejection of Attractive Gambles, Loss Aversion, and the Lemon Avoidance Heuristic. *Journal of Economic Psychology* 29, 715–23.

Fallacy Files. 2010. Available online at http://www.fallacyfiles.org (accessed September 12, 2012).

Flyvbjerg, B. 2005. Design by Deception. The Politics of Megaproject Approval. *Harvard Design Magazine* Spring–Summer, 50–59.

Flyvbjerg, B. 2006. From Nobel Prize to Project Management: Getting Risks Right. *Project Management Journal* August, 5–15.

Forbes. 2008. Shalva Chigirinsky. Available online at http://www.forbes.com/lists/2008/10/billionaires08_Shalva-Chigirinsky_1KH0.html (accessed September 12, 2012).

Forbes. 2012. The World's Billionaires 2012. Available online at http://www.forbes.com/lists/ (accessed September 12, 2012).

Fortune. 2007. 101 Dumbest Moments in Business. Available online at http://money.cnn.com/galleries/2007/fortune/0712/gallery.101_dumbest.fortune/37.html (accessed September 12, 2012).

Fortune. 2012. 100 Best Companies to Work For. Available online at http://money.cnn.com/magazines/fortune/rankings/ (accessed February 20, 2012).

Fowler, J.H. and Christakis, N.A. 2009. Dynamic Spread of Happiness in a Large Social Network: Longitudinal Analysis Over 20 Years in the Framingham Heart Study. *British Medical Journal* 338(768).

Francis, L.J. 1999. Happiness is a Thing Called Stable Extraversion: A Further Examination of the Relationship between the Oxford Happiness Inventory and Eysenck's Dimensional Model of Personality and Gender. *Personality and Individual Differences* 26, 5–11.

Gilbert, D. 2006. *Stumbling on Happiness*. New York: Knopf.

Glasser, J. 2009. America's High-speed Rail off to a Slow Start. *Fortune*. August 6. Available online at http://money.cnn.com/2009/08/05/news/obama_high_speed_rail.fortune/index.htm?postversion=2009080610 (accessed September 12, 2012).

Godin, S. 2005. *All Marketers are Liars: The Power of Telling Authentic Stories in a Low-Trust World*. New York: Portfolio Hardcover.

Goldstein, D.G. and Gigerenzer, G. 1999. The Recognition Heuristic: How Ignorance Makes Us Smart. In G. Gigerenzer and P.M. Todd (eds), *Simple Heuristics That Make Us Smart*. Oxford: Oxford University Press.

Goleman, D. 2006. *Emotional Intelligence: Why It Can Matter More Than IQ*. 10th anniversary edition. New York: Bantam.

Google Inc. 2010. Google Code of Conduct. Available online at http://investor.google.com/conduct.html (accessed September 12, 2012).

Hagberg, E. 2008. The Worst Building in the History of Mankind. *Esquire*. January. Available online at http://www.esquire.com/the-side/DESIGN/hotel-of-doom-012808 (accessed November 8, 2009).

Hall, D. 2005. Lessons Discovered but Seldom Learned, or Why Am I Doing This if No One Listens? In *Proceedings of Space Systems Engineering and Risk Management Symposiums*. Los Angeles, CA, 170–78.

Hammond, J., Keeney, R. and Raiffa, H. 2002. *Smart Choices: A Practical Guide to Making Better Decisions*. New York: Broadway Books.

Harford, T. 2008. *The Logic of Life*. New York: Random House.

Harinck, F., Van Dijk, E., Van Beest, I. and Mersmann, P. 2007. When Gains Loom Larger than Losses: Reversed Loss Aversion for Small Amounts of Money. *Psychological Science* 18, 1099–105.

Harrabin, R. 2007. Climate Change Goal 'Unreachable'. *BBC News*. Available online at http://news.bbc.co.uk/2/hi/science/nature/7135836.stm (accessed September 12, 2012).

Hauser, J. 2007. *Inside the Yellow Pages: A Revealing Look into Directory Publishing and Tips for Creating More Effective Ads, Explained by a Former Yellow Page Salesman*. Charleston, SC: BookSurge Publishing.

Hauser, J. 2010. How Much Should You Spend on Your Yellow Page Advertising Budget? *EZineArticles*. Available online at http://ezinearticles.com/?How-Much-Should-You-Spend-on-Your-Yellow-Page-Advertising-Budget?&id=147774 (accessed March 11, 2010).

Heldman, K. 2005. *Project Manager's Spotlight on Risk Management*. Alameda, CA: Harbor Light Press.

Higbee, K.L. 2001. *Your Memory: How It Works and How to Improve It*. 2nd edition. Cambridge, MA: Da Capo Press.

Hills, P. and Argyle, M. 2002. The Oxford Happiness Questionnaire: A Compact Scale for the Measurement of Psychological Well-being. *Personality and Individual Differences* 33, 1073–82.

Hillson, D. and Murrey-Webster, R. 2007. *Understanding and Managing Risk Attitude*. 2nd edition. Aldershot, UK: Gower Publishing.

Hillson, D. and Murrey-Webster, R. 2008. *Managing Group Risk Attitude*. Aldershot, UK: Gower Publishing.

Hitchings, B. 1979. *Westgate*. Coolah, NSW, Australia: Outback Press.

House, Subcommittee on Manned Space Flight of the Committee on Science and Astronautics. 1974. NASA Authorization, Hearings on H.R. 4567, 93/2, Part 2, p. 1271.

Hunter, I.M.L. 1964. *Memory*. Middlesex, England: Penguin Books.

Huntington Post. 2008. Spitzer's Resignation Speech: Transcript. Available online at http://www.huffingtonpost.com/2008/03/12/spitzers-resignation-spee_n_91157.html (accessed September 12, 2012).

Ig Nobel. 2010. Improbable Research: Research That Makes People Laugh. Available online at http://www.ignobel.com (accessed September 12, 2012).

Insprucker, J. 2008. Sometimes Your Top Ten Risk List Should Include Eleven. In *Proceedings of 2008 Space Systems Engineering and Risk Management Symposium*. February 26–9. Los Angeles, California.

Jacoby, L.L. 1978. On Interpreting the Effects of Repetition: Solving a Problem versus Remembering a Solution. *Journal of Verbal Learning and Verbal Behavior* 17, 649–67.

Janis, I.L. 2008. *Groupthink*. 2nd edition. Boston: Houghton Mifflin.

Kahneman, D. 1999. Objective Happiness. In D. Kahneman, E. Diener and N. Schwarz (eds), *Well-Being: The Foundations of Hedonic Psychology*. New York: Russell Sage, 3–25.

Kahneman, D. 2011. *Thinking Fast and Slow*. New York: Farrar, Straus and Giroux.

Kahneman, D. and Tversky, A. 1979. Prospect Theory: An Analysis of Decisions under Risk. *Econometrica* 47, 263–91.

Kahneman, D., Knetsch, J.L. and Thaler, R.H. 1991. Anomalies: The Endowment Effect, Loss Aversion, and Status Quo Bias. *Journal of Economic Perspectives* 5(1), 193–206.

Kashdan, T.D. 2004. The Assessment of Subjective Well-being (issues raised by the Oxford Happiness Questionnaire), *Personality and Individual Differences* 36, 1225–32.

Kendrick, T. 2009. *Identifying and Managing Project Risk: Essential Tools for Failure-Proofing Your Project*. 2nd edition. New York: AMACOM.

Kluger, J. 2006. Why We Worry about the Things We Shouldn't … and Ignore the Things We Should. *Time* November 26.

Kolesnikov, A. No Survivors. It is Impossible. *Commersant*. August 22.

Komarnicki, J. 2007. Divided Greyhound Workers Narrowly Approve Contract. *Calgary Herald* May 26.

Kutsch, E. and Hall, M. 2009. The Rational Choice of Not Applying Project Risk Management in Information Technology Projects. *Project Management Journal* 40(3), 72–81.

Kwak, Y.H. 2008. Evaluating Project Management Effectiveness of Boston Big Dig and Three Gorges Dam in China. In D. Cleland and L. Ireland (eds), *Project Manager's Handbook*. New York: McGraw-Hill.

Lafleur, C. 2010. Costs of US Piloted Programs. Available online at http://www.thespacereview.com/article/1579/1 (accessed September 12, 2012).

Levinsky, A. 2003. Spacesuit for the Tunnel: Severomuysky Tunnel. *Popular Mechanic*. Available online at http://www.popmech.ru/article/4796-skafandr-dlya-tonnelya/ (accessed September 12, 2012).

Levitt, S. and Dubner, S.J. 2009. *Superfreakonomics: Global Cooling, Patriotic Prostitutes, and Why Suicide Bombers Should Buy Life Insurance*. New York: William Morrow/HarperCollins.

Lichtenstain, S. and Fischhoff, B. 1977. Do Those Who Know More also Know More about How Much They Know? *Organizational Behavior and Human Performance* 20, 159–83.

Linkov, I., Satterstrom, F.K., Kiker, G., Seager, T.P., Bridges, T., Benjamin, S.L. and Belluck, D.A. 2006. From Optimization to Adaptation: Shifting Paradigms in Environmental Management and Their Application to Remedial Decisions. *Integrated Environmental Assessment and Management* 2(1), 92–8.

Loftus, E.F. and Palmer, J.C. 1974. Reconstruction of Automobile Destruction: An Example of the Interaction between Language and Memory. *Journal of Verbal Learning and Verbal Behavior* 13, 585–9.

Lord, C., Ross, L. and Lepper, M. 1979. Biased Assimilation and Attitude Polarization: The Effects of Prior Theories on Subsequently Considered Evidence. *Journal of Personality and Social Psychology* 37, 2098–109.

Lykken, D. and Tellegen, A. 1996. Happiness is a Stochastic Phenomenon. *Psychological Science* 7, 186–9.

Lynch, D.K. 2008. Asteroid Impacts on Earth: Risks and Responsibilities. In *Proceedings of 2008 Space Systems Engineering and Risk Management Symposium.* February 26–9. Los Angeles, California.

Lyubomirsky, S., Schkade, D. and Sheldon, K.M. 2005. Pursuing Happiness: The Architecture of Sustainable Change. *Review of General Psychology* 9(2), 111–31.

Manifesto for Agile Software Development. 2006. Available online at http://agilemanifesto.org (accessed February 1, 2010).

Martin, P. 2009. Money Can Buy You Love, Economist Says. *Sydney Morning Herald* November 16.

Mather, M. and Johnson, M.K. 2000. Choice-supportive Source Monitoring: Do Our Decisions Seem Better to Us as We Age? *Psychology and Aging* 15, 596–606.

McComas, K. 2010. Psychological Factors Influencing How People React to Risk Information. Available online at http://smas.chemeng.ntua.gr/miram/files/publ_311_11_2_2005.pdf (accessed September 12, 2012).

McDonald, L.G. and Robinson, P. 2009. *A Colossal Failure of Common Sense: The Inside Story of the Collapse of Lehman Brothers.* New York: Crown Business.

Mercedes-Benz USA. 2010. Mercedes-Benz Posts Highest Sales Month for the Year with 20,025 Vehicles Sold in December. Mercedes-Benz USA. Press Release 5 January. Available online at http://www.prnewswire.com/news-releases/mercedes-benz-posts-highest-sales-month-for-the-year-with-20025-vehicles-sold-in-december-80710637.html (accessed September 12, 2012).

Mercino, A. 2007. *Emotional Intelligence for Project Managers: The People Skills You Need to Achieve Outstanding Results.* New York: AMACOM.

Merton, R.K. 1968. *Social Theory and Social Structure.* New York: Free Press.

MillwardBrown Optimor. 2011. BRANDZ: Top 100 Most Influential Brands. Available online at http://www.millwardbrown.com/BrandZ/Top_100_Global_Brands/Previous_Years_Results/2011.aspx (accessed September 12, 2012).

MindTools. 2010. Memory Improvement Techniques. Available online at http://www.mindtools.com/memory.html (accessed September 12, 2012).

Mitchell, T. and Thompson, L. 1994. A Theory of Temporal Adjustments of the Evaluation of Events: Rosy Prospection & Rosy Retrospection. In C. Stubbart, J. Porac and J. Meindl (eds), *Advances in Managerial Cognition and Organizational Information-Processing*, Vol. 5. Greenwich, CT: JAI Press, 85–114.

Moskowitz, C. 2010. Five Things That Will Make You Happier. *LiveScience* 22 February. Available online at http://www.livescience.com/health/how-to-be-happy-100222.html (accessed September 12, 2012).

MSNBC News. 2010. Armstrong: Obama NASA Plan 'Devastating'. Available online at http://www.msnbc.msn.com/id/36470363/ns/nightly_news/ (accessed September 12, 2012).

Myers, D.G. 2007. *Social Psychology*. 9th edition. New York: McGraw-Hill.

Nast, J. 2006. *Idea Mapping: How to Access Your Hidden Brain Power, Learn Faster, Remember More, and Achieve Success in Business*. Hoboken, NJ: Wiley.

National Institute of Standards and Technology (NIST). 2002. Press Release: Software Errors Cost U.S. Economy $59.5 Billion Annually. NIST Assesses Technical Needs of Industry to Improve Software-Testing. Available online at http://www.cse.buffalo.edu/~mikeb/Billions.pdf (accessed September 12, 2012).

Nationmaster. 2010. Health Statistics. Available online at http://www.nationmaster.com/graph/hea_phy_per_1000_peo-physicians-per-1-000-people (accessed September 12, 2012).

Paivio, A. 1971. *Imagery and Verbal Processes*. New York: Holt, Rinehart & Winston.

Paivio, A. 1986. *Mental Representations: A Dual-coding Approach*. New York: Oxford University Press.

Pasternak, B. 1997. *Doctor Zhivago*. New York: Pantheon.

Pavot, W. and Diener, E. 1993. Review of the Satisfaction with Life Scale. *Psychological Assessment* 5, 164–72.

Pentagon. 2012. Facts and Figures. Available online at http://pentagon.osd.mil/facts-area.html (accessed September 12, 2012).

Plous, S. 1993. *The Psychology of Judgment and Decision Making*. New York: McGraw-Hill.

Project Management Institute. 2013. *A Guide to the Project Management Body of Knowledge (PMBOK® Guide)*. 5th edition. Newtown Square, PA: Project Management Institute.

Project Management Institute. 2010. *PMI Today* September.

Pronin, E., Lin, D.Y. and Ross, L. 2002. The Bias Blind Spot: Perceptions of Bias in Self versus Others. *Personality and Social Psychology Bulletin* 28, 369–81.

RIA Novosti News Agency. 2012. Bulava "De Facto" Enters Service – Navy Chief. Available online at http://en.rian.ru/trend/bulava_121109/ (accessed September 12, 2012).

Roediger, H.L., Meade, M.L. and Bergman, E. 2001. Social Contagion of Memory. *Psychonomic Bulletin & Review* 8, 365–71.

Roediger, H.L. and McDermott, K.B. 1995. Creating False Memories: Remembering Words Not Presenting in Lists. *Journal of Experimental Psychology. Learning, Memory, and Cognition* 21, 803–14.

Romer, J. 2007. *The Great Pyramid: Ancient Egypt Revisited*. Cambridge: Cambridge University Press.

Ross, L., Greene, D. and House, P. 1977. The False Consensus Effect: An Egocentric Bias in Social Perception and Attribution Processes. *Journal of Experimental Social Psychology* 13, 279–301.

Roth, D. 2009. Time Your Attack: Oracle's Lost Revolution. *Wired Magazine*. December 21.

Russo, J.E. and Schoemaker, P.J.H. 1989. *Decision Traps: Ten Barriers to Brilliant Decision-Making and How to Overcome Them*. New York: Simon & Schuster.

Samuelson, W. and Zeckhauser, R.J. 1988. Status Quo Bias in Decision Making. *Journal of Risk and Uncertainty* 1, 7–59.

Saporito, B. 2002. How Fastow Helped Enron Fall. *Time* February 10.

Schkade, D.A. and Kahneman, D. 1998. Does Living in California Make People Happy? A Focusing Illusion in Judgments of Life Satisfaction. *Psychological Science* 9, 340–46.

Schuyler, J. 2001. *Risk and Decision Analysis in Projects*. 2nd edition. Newtown Square, PA: Project Management Institute.

Schwartz, B. 2005. *The Paradox of Choice: Why More is Less*. New York: Harper Perennial.

Schwarz, T. 2012. North Korea Rocket Breaks Up in Flight. Available online at http://www.cnn.com/2012/04/12/world/asia/north-korea-launch/index.html (accessed September 12, 2012).

Sidoli, M. 1996. Farting as a Defense against Unspeakable Dread. *Journal of Analytical Psychology* 41(2), April, 165–78(14).

Skinner, D. 2009. *Introduction to Decision Analysis*. 3rd edition. Gainesville, FL: Probabilistic Publishing.

Sloan, H.E. 2001. *Principle and Interest: Thomas Jefferson and the Problem of Debt (Jeffersonian America)*. Charlottesville, VA: University of Virginia Press.

Slovic, P. 1987. Perception of Risk. *Science* 236, 280–85.

Slovic, P., Fischhoff, B. and Lichtenstein, S. 1982. Facts versus Fears: Understanding Perceived Risk. In D. Kahneman, A. Tversky, and P. Slovic (eds), *Judgment under Uncertainty: Heuristics and Biases*. Cambridge: Cambridge University Press.

Star Trek. 2010. Borgs. Available online at http://www.startrek.com/startrek/view/library/aliens/article/70558.html (accessed February 19, 2010).

Staw, B.M., Sutton, R.I. and Pelled, L.H. 1994. Employee Positive Emotion and Favorable Outcomes at the Workplace. *Organization Science* 5(1), February, 51–71.

Swanson, L.W. and Petrovich, G.D. 1998. What is the Amygdala? *Trends in Neurosciences* 21(8).

Thaler, R.H. and Sunstein, C.R. 2007. *Nudge. Improving Decisions about Health, Wealth, and Happiness.* New Haven and London: Yale University Press.

Thompson, M. 2010. The Rise and Fall of a Female Captain Bligh. *Times Magazine.* March 3.

Titanic-titanic.com. 2010. Comparing Titanic with Modern Ships and Cruise Liners. Available online at http://www.titanic-titanic.com/compare_modern_ships_to_titanic.shtml (accessed September 12, 2012).

Tonello, M. 2009. *Bringing Home the Birkin: My Life in Hot Pursuit of the World's Most Coveted Handbag.* New York: Harper Paperbacks.

TransCanada. 2012. Keystone Pipeline System. Available online at http://www.transcanada.com/oil-pipelines-projects.html (accessed September 12, 2012).

Tversky, A. and Kahneman, D. 1971. Belief in the Law of Small Numbers. *Psychological Bulletin* 76, 105–10.

Tversky, A. and Kahneman, D. 1973. Availability: A Heuristic for Judging Frequency and Probability. *Cognitive Psychology* 5, 207–32.

Tversky, A. and Kahneman, D. 1974. Judgment under Uncertainty: Heuristics and Biases. *Science* 185, 1124–30.

Tversky, A. and Kahneman, D. 1981. The Framing of Decisions and the Psychology of Choice. *Science* 211, 453–8.

Tversky, A. and Kahneman, D. 1983. Extension versus Intuitive Reasoning: The Conjunction Fallacy in Probability Judgment. *Psychological Review* 90(4), 293–315.

Vedantam, S. 2008. Older Americans May Be Happier Than Younger Ones. *Washington Post* July 14.

Virine, L. and Trumper, M. 2007. *Project Decisions, The Art and Science.* Vienna, VA: Management Concepts.

von Winterfeldt, D. 2008. Should We Protect Commercial Airplanes Against Surface-to-Air Missile Attacks by Terrorists. In *Proceedings of INFORMS Annual Meeting*, Washington, DC, October 12–15.

Walters, C. 1986. *Adaptive Management of Renewable Resources.* New York: Macmillan.

Watson, P.C. 1960. On the Failure to Eliminate Hypotheses in a Conceptual Task. *Quarterly Journal of Experimental Psychology* 12, 129–40.

Weinstein, N. 1989. Optimistic biases about personal risks. *Science*, 246, 1232–3.

Wessel, D. 2009. *In FED We Trust: Ben Bernanke's War on the Great Panic*. New York: Crown Business.

Whalen, P.J. and Phelps, E.A. (eds) 2009. *The Human Amygdala*. New York: The Guilford Press.

Widman, J. 2008. IT's Biggest Project Failures and What We Can Learn From Them. *Computerworld* October 9.

Wrong Diagnosis. 2008. Statistics about Electrocution. Available online at http://www.wrongdiagnosis.com/e/electrocution/stats.htm#medical_stats (accessed September 12, 2012).

Wycoff, J. 1991. *Mindmapping: Your Personal Guide to Exploring Creativity and Problem-Solving*. New York: Berkley Trade.

Yates, F.A. 2001. *The Art of Memory*. Chicago: University of Chicago Press.

Zeigarnik, B. 1967. On Finished and Unfinished Tasks. In W.D. Ellis (ed.), *A Sourcebook of Gestalt Psychology*. New York: Humanities Press.

Index

Page numbers in **bold** refer to instances where the term is defined.

If you have found this book useful you may be interested in other titles from Gower

Benefit Realisation Management
A Practical Guide to Achieving Benefits Through Change
Gerald Bradley
Hardback: 978-1-4094-0094-3
e-book PDF: 978-1-4094-1086-7
e-book ePUB: 978-1-4094-5876-0

Enterprise Growth Strategy
Vision, Planning and Execution
Dhirendra Kumar
Hardback: 978-0-566-09198-8
e-book PDF: 978-0-566-09199-5
e-book ePUB: 978-1-4094-5969-9

MisLeadership
Prevalence, Causes and Consequences
John Rayment and Jonathan Smith
Hardback: 978-0-566-09226-8
e-book PDF: 978-0-566-09227-5
e-book ePUB: 978-1-4094-5974-3

Project Governance
Ralf Müller
Paperback: 978-0-566-08866-7
e-book PDF: 978-0-566-09156-8
e-book ePUB: 978-1-4094-5845-6

GOWER

Project Success
Critical Factors and Behaviours
Emanuel Camilleri
Hardback: 978-0-566-09228-2
e-book PDF: 978-0-566-09229-9
e-book ePUB: 978-1-4094-5896-8

Project-Oriented Leadership
Ralf Müller and J. Rodney Turner
Paperback: 978-0-566-08923-7
e-book PDF: 978-1-4094-0939-7
e-book ePUB: 978-1-4094-5881-4

Rethinking Management
Radical Insights from the Complexity Sciences
Chris Mowles
Hardback: 978-1-4094-2933-3
e-book PDF: 978-1-4094-2934-0
e-book ePUB: 978-1-4094-8674-9

Visit **www.gowerpublishing.com** and

- search the entire catalogue of Gower books in print
- order titles online at 10% discount
- take advantage of special offers
- sign up for our monthly e-mail update service
- download free sample chapters from all recent titles
- download or order our catalogue